GHOSTS
OF LONDON

GHOSTS
OF LONDON

JONATHAN SUTHERLAND

breedon **books**
PUBLISHING

First published in Great Britain in 2002 by
The Breedon Books Publishing Company Limited
Breedon House, 3 The Parker Centre,
Derby, DE21 4SZ.

Dedication

For Uncle Chris

ISBN 1 85983 269 5

Printed and bound by Butler & Tanner, Frome, Somerset, England.

Cover printing by Lawrence Allen.

Contents

Acknowledgements

I am particularly grateful to Chris Leggett who, during the writing of this book, continually provided new leads and information regarding the current state of some of the haunted sites. Chris also made an exceptionally good job of the photography. My thanks, as always, to my partner, Diane, whose dedication and support continue to inspire me. Thanks are also due in part to those who have trodden this path before, despite the fact that their descriptions and conclusions have often only managed to confuse me all the more!

Introduction

Writing this book, which appeared to be a relatively simple task in comparison to the collation of over 2,000 haunted sites for *Ghosts of Great Britain*, became a far more difficult task, but was equally fascinating.

Having lived in London for over 20 years, and having visited many of the sites mentioned in this book, I must nevertheless confess that at the time, apart from some of the more obvious historical locations, I was blissfully unaware of the degree of ghostly activity in the capital.

I thought that I had discovered the majority of hauntings in London while researching *Ghosts of Great Britain*. In fact, I had only seen the tip of the iceberg. Further research has revealed numerous other haunted sites of greater importance and degrees of perplexity than I could have possibly imagined. There are a number of hauntings in this book that will no doubt already be known to many readers. These are the stories that are interwoven into the very fabric of the history of the capital and the country. Rubbing shoulders with these major historical characters are a number of less well-known individuals whose apparitions are just as significant and interesting.

In establishing the geographical parameters of this book I have taken the very liberal view that London is contained within the orbit of the M25. While I apologise to those who live in Essex, Surrey or Kent, for example, for including them in a book focussing on London, it seemed that since these locations' histories were so entwined with that of London that it made sense to bring them together.

Having now completed my second book about ghosts I am still continually asked whether I believe in them. Like most people, the answer is that I am not really sure. I cannot explain some of the things that people have seen and heard, nor can I understand how it has affected them. However, whether you believe these stories or not is not really the point. Some of them are excellent tales in their own right, and I feel that many of the hauntings fill in some of the missing parts of a historical jigsaw that will never be completed. It is simply impossible to believe, unless some of the witnesses are incredibly good at deception, that they would concoct stories for no possible financial or other gain. With the exception of a handful of stories, which will become obvious to you as you read them, none of the witnesses stood to benefit from making up a ghostly encounter. In fact, many of the witnesses would have preferred not to have experienced the hauntings they did. This is what is so confusing about ghostly encounters. Those who actively seek to witness hauntings do not often experience them. Many manifestations appear to people when they least expect it, and usually when they know nothing about it. Witnesses walk into a situation with no prior knowledge of a haunting associated with that location, yet later accurately describe an encounter that mirrors the experiences of others over the years. It is likely that significant numbers of ghostly encounters go unreported, and the phenomena are probably far more common than we know.

Several explanations have been offered to explain ghostly phenomena. It appears that ghosts can manifest themselves in almost any place. A location does not have to be a castle, or a religious building, but can be somewhere that has no particular historical significance. The structures do not seem to have had to have been there for any significant length of time. We have clear examples of this in the fact that even post-war houses can be haunted. Some hauntings seem to keep up a continuous level of intensity or periodic reoccurrence, while others build up over a period of time and become incredibly intense before dying away again. This may mean that we are not dealing with one phenomenon alone, but various different forms of manifestation, perhaps more than we are aware of at present. The term 'haunting' is not particularly well-defined.

One such alternative to a conventional haunting is the poltergeist. There are several examples of poltergeist activity in this book, but they do not follow a regular pattern, despite having some characteristics in common. Poltergeist activity tends to happen in times of trauma, such as a death or divorce. Poltergeists also seem to have some link with adolescent females entering puberty and menopausal women. Some of them actually move around and follow the person that appears to be at the centre of the activity and these people have been described as being like the 'powerhouse' of the phenomenon. There is certainly much that we do not yet understand about psychic energy, altered states of mind and certain parts of the brain. Poltergeists do not always do the same things. Some move things around or throw them, while others can transport objects, make them disappear and then reappear, create fires, write on walls, make banging noises, throw people around or levitate them. Some poltergeists can be driven away or reduced in intensity by religious, spiritual or scientific interference, but this is not always the case.

One of the more plausible explanations for hauntings in general developed from work done by Vic Tandy, an expert in Computer Assisted Learning at Coventry University. His research seems to imply that most ghostly activity experienced by witnesses is as a result of low-frequency sound waves being trapped in buildings. These sound waves cannot be heard by the human ear but could be triggered off by the merest hint of wind impacting the walls. He carried out research in the cellar of a 14th-century building in Coventry that is now Coventry's tourist information centre. Using a sound-level meter with a microphone capable of picking up frequencies as low as 1Hz, he registered infrasound at 19Hz and a level of 38 decibels, which is inaudible to humans. Sounds at these frequencies can create both unease and a feeling of nausea, mimicking the feelings of terror and cold that witnesses often associate with a haunting. These low-frequency sounds can also fool the brain into believing that it has seen a strange apparition. Vic Tandy records in his own notes an encounter he experienced when working in his office at Coventry University one night:

> I began to feel increasingly uncomfortable. I was sweating but cold, and the feeling of depression was noticeable – but there was also something else. It was as though someone was in the room with me. Then I became aware that I was being watched, and a figure slowly emerged to my left. It was indistinct and on the periphery of my vision, but it moved just as I would expect a person to. It was grey, and made no sound. The hair was standing up on the back of my neck – I was terrified.

When he looked up it faded and vanished. He experimented with a fencing blade that he rigged up to see if he could pick up low-frequency sound waves. Sure enough, when he returned to look at the blade after a short period it was vibrating, which gave him the notion that there was air moving around in the room and bouncing off the metal, yet it was so weak that he could not feel it. He pinpointed the source of the air to an extractor fan and after modifying the mount of the fan the effect ceased. Sharing his findings with the Society for Psychical Research, they confirmed that infrasound, as it is called, can create breathlessness, fear and shivering. Meanwhile research by NASA, the American space agency, has shown that the human eyeball similarly vibrates if it encounters infrasound. This causes a 'smearing' of vision.

What these new theories cannot explain are the many cases in which manifestations have actually interacted with witnesses. Neither do they explain poltergeist activity or the fact that many witnesses claim to have seen precisely the same thing as someone else, without prior knowledge of that encounter. The debate will continue.

Personally I do not feel that attempting to obtain a scientific explanation for ghostly manifestations undermines their mystique and excitement, or resolves the confusion that surrounds the whole issue. Attempts to explain hauntings have in no way discouraged the many tourists that flock to London and enjoy the burgeoning ghost-walk industry that has sprung up along the most trodden routes.

I will leave it up to you, the reader, to decide. I do hope, however, that whatever your final opinion, you enjoy reading this book.

Jonathan Sutherland

A-Z of Ghosts

Acton, W3: St Dunstan's Church

This site has had religious connections since the monks of the order of St Bartholomew lived here in the Middle Ages. Ghostly monks have been seen walking up the central aisle of the church, as many as 10 or 12 at a time. It is thought that their appearances come in four-yearly cycles, always accompanied by beautiful chanting and music of a bygone age.

Addington, Surrey: the former Addington Palace, Bishop's Walk/Gravel Hill

Set in 163 acres of land, this site's history pre-dates the Domesday Book. During the 1800s six archbishops of Canterbury lived here and it is believed that Henry VIII courted Anne Boleyn in a hunting lodge that once stood on the site. The palace was initially established as a manor house before the Norman conquest but became a palace in the mid-1770s. It was the brainchild of Barlow Trecothic, who was an alderman in the city of London. He built the Palladian-style residence as his country mansion. Five of the six archbishops are buried in the churchyard of St Mary's Church, Addington, the mansion having become their country retreat in around 1807. Capability Brown designed the gardens. Archbishop Edward White Benson is said to haunt the former Addington Palace, although very little is known of the specifics of the apparition. Archbishop Benson was archbishop of Canterbury and one of the many people interested in investigating the supernatural in the middle of the 19th century. He was one of the founders of the Ghost Society.

The surrounding countryside has a much later ghost. During World War Two a German pilot was killed when he bailed out of his aircraft and his apparition haunts the area.

'Digger Harry' haunts nearby Beare's Wood. Harry was brought to trial for the murder of his wife, although she had died of old age. He had buried her close to his run-down cottage so that he could still be with her. He served six months in prison but by the time he returned home he had forgotten where he had buried her and he died of a broken heart. His apparition has been seen on many occasions, presumably still searching for the site of his wife's burial.

Aldgate underground station, EC3

Inexplicable noises in the form of footsteps and whistling sounds have been heard in the tunnels of this underground station. There have also been reports of the sighting of an apparition of a woman, although it is not known who she is or why she haunts the station. One engineer, while working on high-voltage equipment with a colleague, saw the grey-haired old woman stroking the other man's head. He seemed unaware of her presence. A short time later he made what could have been a fatal error in the course of his work, but rather than dying from the electric shock he received, he was merely knocked unconscious and suffered no long-term ill effects. The log held at the station records all the sightings of the woman, and reports the noises heard by witnesses.

Argyll Street, W1: The London Palladium

The apparition of a beautiful woman dressed in a crinoline gown haunts the old crimson staircase. There are several theories as to who the woman is. Some believe that she is the ghost of Helen Campbell, who lived here when the building was Argyll House. Others believe that she is more likely to be the apparition of a former actress, as the staircase was constructed as part of the theatre and did not exist in Argyll House. Alternatively, she could be Helen Shireburn, who was the mistress of the Duke of Argyll during the time he lived at the house between 1750 and 1762.

Baker Street, W1: No.228

Sarah Siddons (1755–1831), the 18th-century English actress, lived here with her husband William while performing at the famous Drury Lane theatre. The site now houses an electric sub-station used by the tube lines. The inspection gallery on the top floor is the approximate location of Sarah's former bedroom. Several engineers have seen her in this location. Her ghost seems to be active during the day and has been seen walking across rooms and through walls.

Baker Street, W1: No.247, The Volunteer

The ghost of Richard Neville, a cavalier during the English Civil War, has been seen in the cellar on a number of occasions. Neville was a royalist and fought on the king's side at the Battle of Naseby in 1645. The pub was built during 1794 on the site of the Neville family farm, which had been destroyed by a fire that also killed all the members of the Neville family in 1654. The manifestation of Richard Neville seems to have first appeared in 1963, when major structural work was undertaken. A door of an alcove opened to reveal a phantom wearing a coat, breeches and stockings. Since then, poltergeist activity has been reported. Lights have been turned on and off and footsteps have been heard around the building.

Bank of England, EC2

Philip Whitehead was employed by the bank but was said to be a forger. He was arrested, convicted and hanged in 1811. The events seemed to unhinge his sister Sarah's mind, and every day for the next 25 years, until she died in 1836, she made a visit to the Bank of England to enquire after her brother. She haunts the small garden in the middle of the building.

No.228, Baker Street, where the 18th-century actress Sarah Siddons is said to appear.

Another bizarre haunting is linked to the building. Many years ago a truly enormous giant of a man worked as a cashier. He seemed to have some morbid fear that his body would be taken by resurrectionists after he had died. Prior to his death he convinced the governors of the bank to allow his body to be buried within the building in order to protect it. They acceded to his wishes and when some alteration work was done long after his death, workmen discovered a lead coffin said to be eight feet long, with a large iron chain wrapped around it. His apparition has been seen and is described as being eight feet tall.

Bank underground station, EC3

The smell of a freshly dug or opened grave is said to emanate from nowhere in this station. Maintenance workers who have experienced the phenomenon have expressed a fear of working the night shift, because the smell is coupled with a strong feeling of sadness, dread and doom. It is not known what the source of this supernatural activity is.

Barnes, SW13: Common Road, Barnes Common

The common is said to be haunted by a ghost dressed in 19th-century prisoner's clothing, complete with broad arrows. The apparition is said to walk out of a pond and pass people out walking at night. The haunting may be related to the tale of an escaped convict who was being treated at nearby Putney hospital. He took the opportunity to escape, but drowned in the pond after a chase. Alternatively, he may have frozen to death after falling into the pond.

Barnes Common is also known as the haunting place of 'Spring Heel Jack'. In 1838 he apparently emerged from the churchyard, spewing blue and white flames from his mouth, and attacked people crossing the common. There has been much written about this character but it is still not known whether this is simply folklore, or whether a haunting actually took place. In any event, Spring Heel Jack's hauntings and attacks stopped as suddenly as they had begun.

Battersea, SW11: Elland Road, Lavender Hill

Shortly before World War Two Henry Robinson, then aged 86, owned this villa, and had lived there for 25 years. With him lived his 27-year-old son Frederick, his school-teacher daughters Lillah and Kate, and his other daughter, Mrs Perkins, a widow with a 14-year-old son named Peter. When reports emerged about strange happenings at the house, Harry Price, a psychic investigator and writer, investigated the case. He paid his first visit to the house on the morning of 19 January, having received reports about poltergeist happenings in the house. On entering the building he saw smashed furniture, wrecked ornaments and broken windows. After an initial meeting with the family, and discovering that the elder Mr Robinson had

The Bank of England has two apparitions, one male and one female.

been sent to an infirmary away from the poltergeist activity, he decided to team up with a reporter from the evening newspaper to investigate the case thoroughly.

The family explained that the occurrences had begun on 29 November, when lumps of coal and pennies began to fall on the roof of the conservatory at the back of the house. It stopped for a few days and then began again in early December. They reported it to the police, believing it to be vandals. A piece of coal hit a constable's helmet, but when he went to investigate he could find no one. On 19 December a washerwoman quitted her job at the house because she was terrified, having found red-hot cinders in the outhouse. Again the family called the police, and as they sat in the kitchen two potatoes were thrown in at them. The following Monday they heard loud bangings from all round the house. The window panel in Mr Robinson's bedroom was smashed, which prompted his removal to the infirmary. A heavy chest of drawers inexplicably lifted and crashed onto the bedroom floor. One of the sisters claimed to have seen the hallstand swaying as if controlled by some strange power. It fell against the stairs and broke into pieces. By this point the women were frightened of staying in the house, and four men, including the local fishmonger and greengrocer, had witnessed the damage done in the bedroom and the kitchen.

The following Friday Price and a reporter from the *Evening News* returned to the house to see the devastation that had been caused by the phenomenon, but unable to witness anything for themselves, they left after about an hour. Peter Perkins was removed from the house, having been identified by the police as the cause of all the problems, and was examined at St John's Hospital, Battersea. Price visited again after the weekend and was told that the manifestations had been as violent as ever, despite the fact that neither male had been in the house. Price searched the house, but apart from the devastation that had been caused, could find nothing. The following day the family left the house, as during the weekend mounted police had been needed to keep crowds away, and on Saturday some local heroes had tried to break into the house and investigate the phenomenon for themselves. The sisters soon decided to return to the house, and on Wednesday a psychic was brought to the house. She was taken into every room and claimed that the building made her feel miserable. In the kitchen she said she felt chilly despite the fact that there was a fire burning in the grate. She stayed in the room and got colder and colder until she started to shiver. Her breathing slowed and her hands were cold to the touch. She was left in the room with Mrs Perkins while Price and the reporter searched the house again. They looked upstairs and when they got to the top floor they heard something fall, but they could not discover anything. They descended and again heard the sound. When they retraced their steps they saw a bar of soap lying on the ground that they could not have missed when they passed just minutes before.

Frederick Robinson returned to the house after a few days and the manifestations ceased. Eventually the elder Mr Robinson died in the infirmary. Price initially believed that ex-soldiers at a nearby psychiatric hospital were using the house for target practice. There had in fact been some friction between the Robinsons and some of the patients, but this did not explain the many breakages that occurred inside the house. Price discounted Peter Perkins as the cause of the disturbances. Apart from the fact that he had been away from the house during some of the occurrences, he could not easily have slipped away to perpetrate any of the more recent happenings. Price began to settle on the idea that someone was trying to frighten the Robinsons out of the house. He was convinced that initially the phenomenon had been caused by the patients in the hospital, but that once the Robinsons had become extraordinarily fraught about what was going on it had developed into something else. As far as Price was concerned, this was a very peculiar case of poltergeist activity.

Frederick Robinson spoke about the episode in 1941 and said:

> The most wonderful piece of psychic phenomena anyone could observe was the dropping of small, white slips of paper on the stairs, and about the rooms. This, by the way, never appeared in the Press for some reason. Held up to the light these slips revealed writing as if done with a pin – the messages were sometimes threatening, and sometimes more sober in character. I recall one night after an unusually loud series of rappings seeing a message on a slip of paper come down from nowhere to fall on my bed. Upon elucidation, I read this: 'I am having a bad time here. I cannot rest. I was born during the reign of William the Conqueror'. The message was signed by the gruesome name of Tom Blood. Sometimes it was Jessie Blood.

Battersea, SW11: Old Battersea House

Mrs Stirling, a writer of ghost stories who died in 1965, was a former owner of this house and reported the sightings experienced in the building. Mrs Stirling was entertaining a friend to tea one day and was about to sit down when she was stopped by the friend, who claimed that the chair in which she was about to sit was already occupied by a gentleman. They were alone in the house. The woman described the man as being dressed in Elizabethan clothes, carrying a sword and having a pointed beard. On another occasion a different friend also witnessed the apparition and from her detailed description it was thought that he was the ghost of the Duke of Marlborough, who apparently often visited the house when it belonged to Viscount Bolingbroke, for whom it had been built.

Battersea, SW11: Old Swan Pub

During the 12th century, the pub that stood on this site was a popular meeting place for watermen and smugglers. Because the city's main transport route was the River Thames, the pubs along the banks of the river were always very busy. The tunnels that ran from the Old Swan to the cellars of Battersea Church are still in existence and it is thought that they were used by smugglers who would store their wares in the cellars and bring them through the tunnels to the pub, and vice versa. An unknown ghost haunted the original pub and although the manifestation has not appeared for some time it is thought to be the apparition of a smuggler or a river traveller.

Bellingham, SE6: Bromley Road

On 2 September 1898 Alice Grant was killed when her bicycle was hit by a brewer's dray. Her apparition can still be seen cycling around the area and is clearly distinguishable. She wears a long, black skirt and a white blouse with puffed sleeves.

Berkeley Square, W1

A sobbing woman, who, it is believed, left her husband for another man and still regrets it, haunts one of the houses in the square. The woman wears a long dress and a wide-brimmed hat and has been seen and heard by both children and adults on a number of occasions.

Berkeley Square, W1: No.50

No.50 Berkeley Square, an 18th-century building, has gained fame internationally as London's most haunted house. Apparently one owner of the house did not live in it. Instead he employed an elderly couple to care for the house, but they had no access to the upper rooms. Twice a year the owner would arrive, lock the elderly couple in the basement and proceed to inspect the upper rooms alone. Only these upper rooms have been the site of unpleasant and frightening apparitions for at least 300 years.

One of No.50's many ghosts is that of a little girl dressed in Scots plaid. She is said to have been either tortured or frightened to death by a wicked nanny. She has been seen wringing her hands in despair and sobbing on the upper floors of the house.

Another ghost here is Adeline, who lived at the house in the 18th century with her uncle. Her screaming ghost has been seen hanging from the window ledge, replaying her last moments as she tried to escape from his advances.

At the end of the 18th century a man named Dupré locked his mad brother in a room (the Haunted Room) at the top of the stairs. The man could only be fed through a hatch in the door. The apparition of a white-faced man with a gaping jaw is still seen. An alternative story exists about the Haunted Room that stems from a very unhappy occupant in the 1850s. A Mr Myers had leased the house, which he

No.50, Berkeley Square, the most haunted house in London.

intended to live in with his new bride. She left him standing at the altar, and he spent the rest of his life as a recluse, living, eating, drinking and sleeping in the Haunted Room.

Deaths have occurred in the house as a result of the sightings in the Haunted Room. The first occurred when a maid had been allocated the room. She went mad and eventually died in hospital. The second was Sir Robert Warboys, who did not believe in ghosts and accepted a challenge to stay in the room. A gunshot was heard in the middle of the night and Sir Robert was found dead of a gunshot wound, despite the fact that there were no guns in the room. Lord Lyttleton was more fortunate when he accepted the challenge to stay in the room. He was not shot at but managed to fire at the ghost, saying that during the night something had leapt out of nowhere toward his bed. Nothing was found in the morning.

During the time when the house was empty, in around 1887, two sailors, desperate for somewhere to sleep, broke into No.50 and settled down in the Haunted Room. They both awoke in the night to a feeling of horror and were aware of a presence in the room. One of the sailors fled the house, unaware of the fact that his mate was trapped in the room with the apparition of the white-faced man with the gaping jaw. The sailor, together with a policeman, watched his friend fall from the window and impale his body on a spiked railing. He died a short time after, his face contorted with fear.

The stories began to decline during the early 20th century when the house became a bookshop. During World War Two staff slept in the upper rooms without encountering any manifestations. The house is still a bookshop and tourists and ghost-hunters commonly visit it. It is said that *A School Story* by M.R. James contains sections based on the house in Berkeley Square.

Berkeley Square, W1: No.53

The apparition seen at this house is said to be the ghost of a man who died of a broken heart. The man's daughter had eloped, but promised her father she would return to their home. She never came back, and it is said that her father still waits in vain for her to appear. His ghost is reported to be a sad and hopeless-looking figure that stares out of one of the windows of the house. He wears a satin coat with lace ruffles at the neck and wrists, and sports a white wig.

Bermondsey, SE1: The Anchor Tap, Horseley Down Lane

A ghost called Charlie is said to haunt this pub. Over the years, several licensees have reported that items have disappeared and then reappeared in strange places. On one particular occasion, a woman's watch disappeared from its normal place on a dressing-room table, only to appear again two months later in the laundry basket. Despite its long disappearance, it was still working and showing the correct time.

Bermondsey, SE1: The Horn Inn, Crucifix Lane

The ghost of an eight-year-old Victorian girl called Mary Isaac haunts this pub. Her spirit has been heard to cry and call for her mother, who died shortly before her. The inn is also haunted by the manifestation of an old woman. She bangs on the floors and walls and moves furniture about.

Bethlehem Hospital (Bedlam), Liverpool Street, Moorfields and Lambeth Road

The Hospital of the Star of Bethlehem was the first mental asylum in London. Originally it was situated on the site of what is now Liverpool Street station, but from 1675 to 1815 it was sited at Moorfields, before being moved to ground on which the Imperial War Museum now stands. During World War Two a barrage balloon unit was stationed in the grounds of the museum, and the crew complained that they heard groans and the rattling of chains. One of the many stories that may explain some of these hauntings relates to 1780. A servant girl called Rebecca fell in love with her master. One day, he decided to move away, and he thanked her for her services and slipped a golden guinea into her hand. This slight sent the girl insane and she was admitted to Bedlam. She spent the rest of her life there, holding the coin and wishing to be buried with it. An attendant prised it from her still-warm fingers when she died. Rebecca's ghost was seen with wild-looking eyes searching for the stolen coin. On more than one occasion attendants and patients were confronted by Rebecca's ghost screaming 'Give me back my guinea!' When the asylum was transferred to Lambeth Road in 1815 the ghost of Rebecca moved with it, still searching for her coin.

Bethnal Green, E2: Teesdale Street

No.132 Teesdale Street has now been demolished, but it was an early Victorian three-storey house which belonged to the Davis family. George Davis's wife had been born there, as had her father. In September 1936 Davis's wife died, having suffered from epilepsy for nearly 30 years. Apparently her legs were very ulcerated toward the end of her life and she was an invalid. The Davis family sub-let the upper floor to the Harrison family, who had an 18-month-old child. They had lived there for five years and helped to look after Mrs Davis during the final weeks of her life. She died in hospital on 12 September and was buried at Manor Park Cemetery. It seems that from then on the house was beset by strange phenomena.

In February 1938 supernatural incidents catapulted the house and its inhabitants into the full glare of the media and the public. The *Evening Standard* even sent a reporter to spend the night in the haunted house. Garry Allighan claimed to have seen and heard a ghost. He interviewed George and his children, Grace and Sidney Davis, who reported hearing tapping noises, moans and heavy footsteps. They also recounted to him that bedroom furniture had been moved and that their bedclothes were frequently thrown onto the floor during the night. Mrs Harrison reported seeing pictures on the wall twisting around and when she tried to stop them from doing so, one of the pictures was snatched from her hand by an invisible force and smashed on the ground. Grace also said that most of the crockery on the dresser in the kitchen was removed and placed on the table nearly every morning. While the reporter was still there he heard a cry, heavy footsteps and a loud crash. On investigating with Mr Davis he confirmed that furniture had been moved and bedclothes pulled off.

During the course of the investigations George Davis resorted to strange and desperate measures to prevent the hauntings. He took to tying chairs to his bed, but in the morning found that the chair was on the floor and the string had disappeared. Such a well-documented haunting attracted the attention of paranormal experts, and Dr Fodor of the International Institute for Cyclical Investigation visited the house on 6 February. While talking to the family he heard bangs and saw pictures that had been moved, furniture that had been overturned and ornaments that had been placed in odd positions. Connections were beginning to be made to the deceased wife. Many of the cries were reminiscent of her outbursts before she went into a fit. Often she would clutch at furniture or objects to steady herself, usually resulting in them falling over or being broken.

Dr Fodor was sceptical about some of the events, and noticed that Mrs Harrison was a dominant personality who could easily influence Mr Davis, her husband and Grace. Until this point the ghost had only actually been seen by the Harrisons. The Davis family had only witnessed the evidence of the visitations. All the inhabitants of the house believed that the ghost was that of Mrs Davis, and that she was trying to force the Harrisons out of the house. However, the investigators, local newspapers and later the national newspapers picked up on the sceptical stance of Dr Fodor and accused the family of manufacturing the paranormal activity. Nevertheless, the house had become notorious, and on one occasion 2,000 people crowded the street, hoping to see something out of the ordinary.

Shortly after this event the psychic investigator, Harry Price, visited Teesdale Street. Lawrence Evans, one of Dr Fodor's assistants, sealed off the front bedroom, where the chair had been tied and many of the noises originated.

In his journal Evans says:

> I then went upstairs into the front room and securely fastened both the windows with 2-inch steel screws, so that neither the top or the bottom could be moved. The Marquis des Barres [another psychic

investigator and friend of Evans] was helping me, and together we marked the position of every piece of furniture in the room by marking the floor in blue pencil exactly under the leg of each piece. I then sprinkled about 2lb of powdered starch on the floor in the vicinity of the door. We took particular care to make no mark on the floor with our own feet, by sprinkling the floor in front of us and backing out of the room. We then shut the door and I took the following precautions to prevent entry. I had obtained 6 1-inch steel screw eyes which I placed in pairs, on the door, and on the lintel in three different places. I then fastened each pair together with 7-22 copper wire. After that I threaded tape through each pair of eyes, wound it round the wire, tied it, and sealed it with my own private seal. I am quite satisfied that it is impossible for normal entry to be made without it being quite apparent to us. As I was coming down the stairs, preparatory to leaving the house, I heard the moan. It appeared to come from below where Grace, Mrs Harrison and the baby were sitting in the kitchen. I asked them if they had heard it also, and they said that they had and that it had come from the front room. I went into the front room and found the glass cover had been taken completely off the near pin cushion and had been placed on the piano beside it, and the glass cover had been slightly moved from the second pin cushion.

Lawrence Evans returned to the house on 10 February, having left the room sealed for two days. The room was untouched. Nevertheless, the family continued to report problems and their sanity and good character, doubted by some, was supported by many neighbours. A Mrs Pierce, who had known the family for 33 years, claimed that 10 or 15 people had seen a picture turning on the mantelpiece. The Revd F.G.S. Nicholle, the local vicar, also heard cries and saw a chair that had been thrown across the back bedroom. He also told Dr Fodor that he had heard tapping sounds and confirmed that all the family and the Harrisons were in the kitchen when it had happened.

Evans now decided to perform the same sealing exercise on the sitting room, having turned the two pictures of Mrs Davis that were on the mantelpiece backwards. One of the pin cushions was placed in Grace's room and the other in the kitchen. When the investigators returned on 11 February Grace claimed that sitting in the kitchen she had seen the pictures turn around and then turn back. Nobody else had seen this.

J. Bardell Smith, an expert in the occult, suggested a reason for the poltergeist activities in the house:

In all poltergeist cases it has been found that there lives in the house a woman in dawning womanhood say from 16–21 years of age; and through some mysterious makeup of her physical body 'power' or energy can be drawn by the 'ghost' to move articles, make noises and other very unpleasant demonstrations. How can these happenings be stopped? The most drastic and certain remedy is the removal of the 'power station' – if the lady of 16–21 leaves the house these ghostly demonstrations will certainly come to an end.

By this point both the Davis family and the Harrisons were looking for somewhere else to live.

Dr Fodor last visited the house on 18 February, a report of which was contained in the *City and East London Observer*:

Upon our arrival, we were met by Mrs Harrison, the tenant who was moving out that day, and conducted into the kitchen where Grace Davis, her two brothers and sister-in-law were sitting. The first question the doctor asked was 'Has anything happened since I was last here?' The reply came from Grace Davis: 'Owing to the publicity we have received I prefer not to say anything about it'. After a while, however, Grace and Mrs Harrison told us the following story 'Last Sunday afternoon we were sitting in this room when Mrs Harrison happened to glance through the communicating door of our front room and saw the outline of a man standing in front of the piano, gazing at an object. She called me and I saw it too,' said Grace. 'Mrs Harrison asked my father to move from the position he was standing in. He did so and the vision still remained. We noticed that my father was in his shirtsleeves, whereas the apparition had a black coat on and a moustache, while my father is clean-shaven. This occurred in broad daylight.' Mrs Harrison here took up the conversation and described once again the sensations she experienced on Friday, when Dr Fodor's assistant and myself persuaded her to lie down on the bed of the late Mrs Davis. She then complained of feeling 'deathly cold', and said she felt as if the back of her head were being pressed in. She seemed to be in a state of coma and clutched at her throat, declaring her mouth and throat were dry and sore. By careful questioning I discovered that Mrs Harrison was the first to see or hear anything untoward happening three months ago. She said, 'I saw the figure of Mrs Davis clearly and the word "go" was uttered distinctly. Immediately after this I visited a London spiritualist who warned me that unless I moved something serious might happen on the middle floor.' A fear has been on the household for some time due to the disappearance of a piece of string from the bedroom of the late Mrs Davis when a chair was tied to the bed and the 'ghost' decided, after several times untying it, to remove it completely. Every member of the household definitely states that this piece of string was not removed by themselves, and they have spent many hours looking for it, owing to fear of strangulation. Mrs Harrison, continuing her conversation stated she had not told anyone of the fact that she had been to a spiritualist. Dr Fodor and myself visited the rooms which, it was suggested, had been disturbed since our last visit and we could find no traces of upheaval. A quick test by the doctor showed no results. He has decided that imagination is playing a part in the later happenings and discounts the theory that the 'ghost' is still present in the house. As far as the new 'vision' is concerned, we discovered that when the house was being built, a man was supposed to have fallen off the scaffolding and was killed. [Mrs Davis's father is the man in question but he actually died after falling while repairing the roof.] Dr Fodor suggested to me that the tenants knowing this, it reacted on their agitated minds, which readily associated the 'vision' with this past occurrence. To demonstrate his theory, he showed me that a person passing or standing outside the house, their shadow would be thrown and reflected through the front window, and owing to the number of glass objects in the room, could possibly be seen in outline. Mrs Harrison leaves the house today (Thursday) and Dr Fodor is convinced that the manifestations will not recur. 'I believe in the first place there was a genuine phenomenon behind it,' said Dr Fodor, summing up his conclusions. 'I refuse to believe all that has happened in the house could be due to imagination alone, neither could it have been a hoax. Many things could be explained but others were inexplicable. The later happenings are, in my opinion, an aftermath of the original manifestations, due to overwrought nerves. It is the well-known last phase of all ghostly disturbances.'

Fodor was still perplexed by the case, and visited the spiritualist that Mrs Harrison had seen the year before. She confirmed to him that she had felt that Mrs Harrison should move before there was any trouble, but this was before the death of Mrs Davis. Mrs Harrison had visited the spiritualist again some six weeks before Christmas. Grace Davis accompanied her. They gave her Mrs Davis's wedding ring; the message was the same. Later the medium had come to the house and had sat in Mrs Davis's chair. The medium's message was even clearer this time. Mrs Davis had apparently thought that Mrs Harrison had stolen money from her when she was still alive and was extremely hostile toward her.

Some light can be shed on Mrs Harrison in a letter that Revd Nicholle wrote to Dr Fodor:

> I could not discover that Mrs Davis had missed any money after her fits, but she did lose several pieces of jewellery about which I gather she had her suspicions. Mrs Harrison was in the habit of running into debt, and of borrowing money and household things, which was a source of annoyance to Mrs Davis. I understand that she is in Mr Davis's debt, and that is why they have not got rid of her before now. Mrs Davis evidently disliked her excessively, and kept saying that there would be no peace in the house while she was in it. There can, I think, be no doubt that Mrs H is the cause of these disturbances, and that their purpose has been either one of hostility, or perhaps of concern for the peace of the family.

Whether the Harrisons hoaxed the incidents in order to escape paying their debts to the Davis family will, perhaps, never be known. Certainly as far as Grace, a good friend of Mrs Harrison was concerned, there was no real trouble between the two families. Unfortunately no further research can be done on this case, since although the Davis family continued to live in the house for nearly 20 years, it was demolished in 1956 and replaced by a block of flats.

Bexley, Kent: Hall Place, Bourne Road

This building dates from 1537 and has a later 17th-century extension, but is believed to be on the site of an older house constructed in the 13th century by the At-Hall family of local aristocrats. However, the ghosts seem to predate the manor house that was built here. A white lady, said to have been the wife of Sir Thomas At-Hall, Lady Constance At-Hall, also haunts the house, but presumably the earlier one. A stag gored Sir Thomas and the distraught Lady Constance not only witnessed the incident but also was so traumatised by it that she climbed to the top of the tower and threw herself to the ground.

Edward the Black Prince also appears in his black armour, accompanied by the sound of mediaeval instruments. His apparition is said to be of particular significance as it foretells a terrible tragedy for the British Army. On four occasions between 1917 and 1943 sightings of his apparition coincided with defeat for Britain. The link with Edward is through his wife, Joan, who was born near here. Prior to leaving for France and Crécy, Edward actually stayed here. In 1347 he lived in Pulteney House on the site of the Coldharbour Palace in London.

Finally, the ghost of a maidservant who is said to have died or have been murdered here haunts the attic area.

In May 2000 a student from the University of Greenwich installed equipment that could detect fluctuations in temperature, light and sound in the basement of the building. He described the findings by saying

> We were definitely feeling some very strange things down there. The readings were going all over the place. The hairs were standing up on the back of my neck. I am definitely convinced that there is something there. This was my first delve into the world of the paranormal and certainly my first time as a ghost-hunter.

Bishopsgate, EC2: St Botolph's Without Bishopsgate Church

During the early 1980s a photographer, Chris Brackley, took a photograph while he was alone in the church with his wife. When the photograph was developed an unexplained figure appeared to be standing on one of the balconies of the church. She was wearing old-fashioned clothing and the photographer and his wife could not explain her appearance in the image. Some years later the photographer was contacted by a workman involved in the restoration of the crypt of the church, who informed him that he had come across a pile of old coffins secreted in the walls of the crypt. On opening one of the coffins the workman recognised the occupant as having a face very similar to that of the woman who had been so mysteriously photographed years before. It appears that by some chance the general facial features had been preserved despite the passing of time. There is no further information as to who this mysterious woman might be.

Blackfriars, EC4: Puddle Dock

The Guildhall Library holds records of extreme poltergeist activity that took place in a building here during the 17th century. Apparently the upper floors of the house were haunted for the same hour each night for more than two weeks. Doors were inexplicably opened and items moved around the house from one room to another. On one occasion the occupier, Mr Edward Pitts, saw a cat-like thing the size of a Mastiff dog sitting on his dresser, which then slid off onto the floor and disappeared.

Blackfriars, SE1: No.1, Stamford Street

In around 1820 a tract was published entitled *The History of the Mysterious House and Alarming Appearances at the Corner of Stamford Street, Blackfriars Road, well-known to have been unoccupied for many years and called The Skeleton's Corner and also the particulars of the female spectre which appeared at the window; and an account of who are the victims of seduction and murder. The Wonder and Excitement Caused by the Appearance of the House, and also by the Curious and Extraordinary Disappearance of the Inmates. Alarming noises and strange shadows; the curiosity exited on passing the house, and an account of what has been reported to have been seen of the Skeleton and Apparitions.* This most intriguing title was published by

W. Jenkinson of 91, Leather Lane, Holborn. In 1820 the house was derelict and simply had the reputation for being evil on account of the fact that it was empty. What is particularly interesting is that several stories of hauntings have been amalgamated into this one case.

At the time the pamphlet was written it seems that the house was not inhabited, at least by mortal souls, but it nevertheless became associated with strange shadows and sounds that perturbed many who passed the building.

> Sometime since, about midnight, the passengers were suddenly surprised by flashes of light appearing at each window, and being known as an empty house of course could not be accounted for, their astonishment was however increased as they became more frequent, and between each flash a low moaning sound like a being in distress struck upon the ear; this was repeated at intervals and a mist was also seen to rise and invelope [sic] the house as almost to hide it from sight, but this clearing off it seemed at rest and as peaceable as ever.

Other witnesses, so the pamphlet claimed, saw more frightening manifestations.

> The astonishment and consternation created one night may be better imagined than described when the spectre of a woman in white without a head was seen at full length at one of the windows, there being no light it could not be so well seen, but it was plain enough to be described; how the head was taken off could not be told, but dressed in a winding sheet it presented a hideous appearance, and scared many away at the time; it soon gradually disappeared, and the figure of a murderous looking villain with a razor in one hand and the head of a female apparently in a handkerchief was seen as if in the act of making an escape.

Not all of the hauntings took place during the night.

> In the day time all the shutters would appear shut, but this cannot be the case at night, when such sights are seen. It is almost impossible to describe all that has been said to have been seen in or about this mysterious dwelling. One account is related of it being once the residence of a rich heiress, who being left without a guardian, was overwhelmed by suitors, and many was the duels fought in her behalf. How many victims fell through their violent passion cannot be told, but the house is supposed to be haunted with their spectres.

Other witnesses claimed to have seen and heard other strange phenomena, such as 'a skeleton with a light', 'a continual tapping at the windows, but nothing visible; it has even been said that the knocker has kept knocking at the door' and even 'a strange looking figure has also been seen to bob its head up the iron plate hole in the street'.

The writer also reminded readers of:

> ...a strange looking lady, inveloped [sic] entirely in black, used to saunter about the Blackfriars Road, and who she was or where she came from nobody ever knew; from one years end to the other her dress was always the same. A year or so since it was reported that this individual died, but it is said that her spirit still hovers about these premises and frequently appears at the windows.

Clearly the writer was not wholly convinced by the supernatural phenomena witnessed by several people.

> It is certainly possible as the eye being at all times likely to be deceived, that second sight developing supernatural antics was brought into practice; but it would be as well to endeavour to fathom the causes of such mysterious accounts, and the following is adduced.
>
> According to one report the house is suddenly illuminated; could this have been by the magic influence of glaring lightening, and the ugly figures might have been the reflection on the glass of the lookers on themselves?
>
> At another time is seen the appearance of a skeleton, this would scare timid persons enough at the time, but persons of stronger nerves would be apt to enquire into the cause of such an appearance. Who knows but at the doctors opposite an anatomical subject may be for surgical science placed in a room opposite to where the identical figure was seen, and the light moved about by the parties pursuing their studies.

Finally he put many of the other apparitions down to pranks designed to frighten or scare away the unwary and suggested that the building was being used for nefarious activities such as prostitution and as a place for street robbers to spy out potential victims. He nevertheless urged readers to 'bestir themselves to go and see it.'

Blackheath, SE3: Hare and Billet Road

The shadowy manifestation of a Victorian figure is thought be that of a woman who had just left her husband and was waiting for her lover, who never arrived. They had planned to elope abroad together. She hanged herself from a nearby elm tree when she realised that she had been stood up.

The ghost of a maidservant called Annie Hawkins is also said to haunt the area. Apparently she was spurned by her lover and committed suicide by drowning herself in the pond.

Blackheath, SE3: Public Library, St John's Park

Elsie Marshall lived here in 1874 during her father's term as a local vicar. She became a missionary and was killed in 1895 by Chinese bandits. However, it seems that she had a particular affinity with the building as her ghost has returned here. The building is now a library and various witnesses have felt her presence brush past them while they browse the books.

Blackwall, E14: Blackwall Tunnel

The tunnel was opened on 22 May 1897 and was, at the time, the longest underwater tunnel in the world. During the construction, which took six years, 641 people living in Greenwich had to be rehoused because their homes were demolished. The cost of this, plus the building of the tunnel itself, provision of lighting and purchase of land, came to £1,400,000. Sir Walter Raleigh once owned one of the demolished houses and it was said that the first pipe ever smoked in England was lit there. Later, the same house was inhabited by Sir John de Pulteney (four times lord mayor of London) and Sebastian Cabot. When the tunnel was built Brunel had only recently invented the shield-tunnelling method, which had been used on an earlier Thames tunnel, now used by the underground. The safety record was good. A tunnel was built under the Hudson River just before work began on the Blackwall Tunnel, and one man per month was killed in the course of construction. There were only seven fatalities during the six years it took to construct the Blackwall Tunnel. As traffic through the tunnel increased, it became apparent that a second tunnel was needed. The second bore took seven years to construct. In October 1972, a motorcyclist offered a lift to a boy from Essex who was hitchhiking on the Greenwich side of the tunnel. By the time they reached the end of the tunnel, the boy had disappeared. The biker sped back to see if he had fallen off, but could find nothing. He went to the boy's house to tell them what had happened and was told that their son had died in the tunnel several years earlier, while riding pillion on a motorbike.

Blackwall, SE10: Millennium Dome, Ordnance Crescent

The ghost of Sir George Livesey, former chairman of the South Metropolitan Gas Works, made an appearance in 2000 in front of astonished workmen attempting to complete the ambitious Dome project. The gas works and its associated offices formerly occupied the site. Sir George was a popular man who died at the beginning of the 20th century. He introduced a profit-sharing scheme for his employees and was generally benevolent toward the poor and needy. Seven thousand people attended his funeral service and burial. If the ghost seen by the workmen in 2000 was that of Sir George, it links neatly with a rumour that after his death he haunted the offices of the gas works. This bearded apparition, which closely resembled Sir George, would apparently wreck people's desks and scatter paperwork everywhere. One can only wonder why Sir George's ghost chose to appear laughing before the Millennium Dome construction workers.

Bloomsbury, WC2: Tavistock Place

Two ghosts are said to meet in unusual circumstances in Tavistock Place. The first sighting of them was in the middle of the 19th century and further sightings have been recorded since then. The apparitions are those of a man and a woman. The man is believed to be the ghost of an undertaker and is wearing a tailcoat and a stovepipe hat with a black ribbon hanging from the back of it. The man stands in Tavistock Place for a while before being approached by a female apparition. She joins him and peers into his face for a while before running away and disappearing into thin air.

Bow, E3: Barton House

This strange case may simply have been an attempt by the residents to force the local authority to rehouse them, but there is no other plausible explanation for the events or sightings. In 1977, when the Greater London Council (GLC) owned the building, the Ussher family occupied one of the flats. For some time they claimed to have seen the manifestation of an old lady wearing a white apron and carpet slippers. To begin with the ghost was only seen, but after a while it began to act as a poltergeist and turned off the electricity at the mains, swept items from shelves and interfered with electrical equipment. Subsequently both a Catholic priest and an Anglican vicar attempted exorcisms; both failed. A medium was only able to tell the family that the apparition was hostile toward them. The building is said to have been built on the site of a convent, but none of the witnesses describe the apparition as looking like a nun. Housing records show that there has never been an old woman living in the flat. Whether this was a real haunting or a hoax may never be known.

Bow, E3: Groveland Court, Bow Lane

A policeman patrolling this area during the evening, accompanied by his dog, experienced a strange phenomenon. The dog suddenly stood rigidly still and began growling incessantly, refusing to move and follow his master into Groveland Court. This is not the only strange event to have taken place in the area. In the 1930s another police constable reported that when he entered the court he felt as if someone had pushed him. The phantom push caused the constable to stumble and he fell to the ground, banging his head on the pavement.

Another ghostly occurence, again in the 1930s, revolved around the pub situated in this court, Williamson's Tavern. The then landlord, William Hollis, experienced poltergeist activity in the form of inexplicable noises that were made regularly on

Saturday evenings. Mr Hollis also saw a manifestation moving over the court itself on a number of occasions, although it is not known what form the shape took. Eventually the ghostly activity in and around the tavern became too much for Mr Hollis and he moved out of the area.

Bow, E3: The Black Swan, Bow Road

A bomb dropped from a Zeppelin in 1916 destroyed the public house. The landlord's mother, two of his daughters and the eldest daughter's baby were killed in the blast. It is no great surprise that Sylvia and Cissie Reynolds, the two daughters, haunt the site of their untimely death. Not only have they been seen in several rooms, especially the cellar, but they may also be responsible for a number of strange incidents. Beer taps have been turned on during the night, causing floods of beer, and a German Shepherd dog kept by the landlord will not go down the stairs to the cellar. The pub is next door to a funeral parlour and some of the customers attribute the strange happenings to this fact.

Bow, E3: The Bow Bells, Bow Road

This public house boasts a 'phantom flusher' in the women's lavatory. Several witnesses have reported that the locked lavatory door has been flung open and an unseen hand has flushed the toilet's cistern. After the landlord experienced icy cold conditions when all the doors were closed, and saw a strange mist rising from the floor, a séance was organised. All that was achieved by this was that the spirit was provoked to storm the door and break a pane of glass in a window.

Brentford, Essex: Boston Manor House, Boston Manor Road

There are conflicting views about the identity of the 'Lady of the Lake' that is seen at Boston Manor House. Some believe the apparition to be that of Lady Boston, who was having an affair with Lord Fairfax. When her husband found out about her indiscretion he murdered her. Others think that the manifestation that glides across the lawn to the lake is that of a Victorian woman who committed suicide when her lover spurned her. Whoever the lady is, she has been seen on numerous occasions, both by the lake and by a cypress tree along the pathway leading to the house. It is, however, possible that two female apparitions haunt this house, each wearing a white, flowing gown. A female skeleton was found inside the grounds surrounding the house and was later re-buried on the estate.

The Mummy's Case, also known as the Mummy's Board, British Museum.

British Museum, WC1

Given the vast number of exhibits in the British Museum, it is rather surprising that there are only two hauntings, and there has only been one inexplicable incident.

The first haunting relates to exhibit 22542, an Egyptian mummy case of the Amon-Ra period. The case is covered in hieroglyphics and has the face of a beautiful singer to the God inscribed on it. It was discovered in the 1880s by English tourists who bought it in Thebes from a trader, and is said to be linked to at least 13 deaths. One of these first owners was injured in a hunting accident the very next day and had to have his arm amputated. Another man vanished in mysterious circumstances and was never seen again. After this the one-armed man sold the mummy case to a dealer in Cairo. Three people then bought it, but they all died and the case was shipped to London. Here it was bought by a collector, who was told by a friend that evil emanated from the case and he should get rid of it. The collector took this advice and sold it on, to a person who had it photographed. The photographer died the following day. It is said that when the photographs were developed, instead of the image of a beautiful woman on the case, an old, evil-looking woman stared straight at the lens.

The case was then bought by a woman who put it in her home. On the first night it was there all her pets died and all the glass in her house shattered. She, despite the attention of medical experts, fell into a coma-like state. In a moment of lucidity she gave the case away and subsequently returned to good health. The mummy case finally found a permanent home in the British Museum in 1889, but the curse was still apparently active. Two porters brought it into the building; one fell and broke his leg and the other died within the week. The case had achieved a high degree of notoriety and it was said that artists that came to draw the case could never do so accurately. At night museum caretakers complained of feeling an evil presence in the room that housed the case. One of them claimed to have seen a manifestation and described it as a hideous yellow-green wrinkled face.

A further death was associated with the case, that of another photographer, who, after developing shots that he had taken of the case, committed suicide. When the body was removed from the case and taken to America it was said to have caused the sinking of the *Empress of Ireland* in the St Lawrence River. In 1921 two psychics attempted to exorcise the case; they described the apparition that emerged from it as having a flat face and a jelly-like body. It leered at them. They believed that the hieroglyphics on the mummy case signified powerful magic and that they had been placed there after the body had been desecrated and removed from the case.

The second manifestation relates to an African mask that is said to have the property of being able to cause deep wounds in anyone that touches it. There does not appear to be any reason why the mask should do this, as it has no sharp edges. It is believed that the object is cursed. The inexplicable incident concerns the remains of Katebit, also housed in the Egyptian Rooms, which are said to be capable of movement. Katebit was a priestess, also of the Amon-Ra period, and witnesses have reported seeing her head move very slowly from one side to the other.

Broadwick Street, W1: The John Snow

The name of this pub is dedicated to the memory of the man who, during the time when a cholera epidemic caused the death of many Londoners, proved that the disease was caused by polluted drinking water. It could be that the ghost that haunts the pub is one of the victims of the disease, although it is not thought that it is John Snow himself. The apparition sits in the corner and stares into space. It is said to have bright red eyes and a contorted face. Witnesses have also reported the feeling of someone brushing past them when they have been alone in the building.

Brook Street, W1

Lord and Lady Clark used to live in one of the houses on this street. He was a doctor, as was their son John, who lived abroad with his wife and their only son. One morning Lady Clark was lying in bed after her husband had gone off to work when her bedroom door opened. As she assumed it was her maid entering the room, she did not look up for quite some time. When she did she was amazed to see the reflection of her son in the mirror. He was carrying the body of a dead child swathed in an Indian scarf that she had given to her daughter-in-law. As she looked at the reflection the image gradually became indistinct and then vanished. When Lord Clark returned to the house his wife told him of the incident and they both decided that she must have been having a dream. However, some time later they received notification from John that his son had died and that because they wanted the boy to be buried in England, his body was being despatched by boat. When the coffin arrived, the child was swathed in the Indian scarf.

Buckingham Palace, SW1

Built by the Duke of Buckingham during the reign of Queen Anne, Buckingham Palace is haunted by the ghost of a monk who died in a punishment cell of the

Buckingham Palace is haunted by a punished monk and gunshots.

Front view, Buckingham Palace, where Major John Gwynne committed suicide.

priory that stood there until 1539. He is said to appear in his brown habit at Christmas, walking in irons on the rear terrace, moaning as he walks up and down for a few minutes before disappearing.

The palace is also haunted by Major John Gwynne, a private secretary to King Edward VII, who committed suicide at the beginning of the 20th century after a divorce scandal. He blew his own brains out in his first-floor office. Phantom gunshots have been heard coming from the area.

Buckingham Street, WC2

Two houses along this street are haunted. No.12 boasts the spirit of Samuel Pepys. He lived here during the Jacobean period and has been seen in the hallway of the house or watching the street from one of the upstairs windows. He is reported to be a friendly and smiling ghost that does not cause those who see him to feel afraid.

No.14, although the house of the Victorian painter William Etty, is not haunted by him but by a happy female ghost, thought to be one of the models that spent countless hours posing for him. Etty was born in York but became a painter in London and was particularly renowned for his nude paintings, some of which are held at the Tate Gallery and the Victoria and Albert Museum.

No.12 Buckingham Street, the former home of Samuel Pepys.

No.14 Buckingham Street boasts the ghost of a former model who sat for the painter William Etty.

Byward Street, EC3: All Hallows-by-the-Tower

This church was restored after it sustained considerable bomb damage during World War Two and is said to be haunted by a Persian cat. The organist, Miss Liscette Rist, was an animal-lover who requested that her pet cat be buried in consecrated ground when it died. Unfortunately this request was denied and the restless spirit of the poor animal now prowls the church.

Camberwell, SE5: Churchyard Passage

St Giles's Church was built in the middle of the 19th century, and is the most recent of five churches that have stood on this site. There is a passage that used to lead to the old Clergy House, but this is now demolished. The ghost of an old clergyman has been seen walking along the passageway; he is thought to be a former vicar.

Cambridge Circus, WC2: The Palace Theatre

Three ghosts reputedly haunt this theatre. The first is that of the much-acclaimed ballerina Anna Pavlova. She lived in Ivy House, now a museum dedicated to her career, from 1913 until she died in 1931. The second ghost is the Welsh-born Ivor Novello, the famous composer, producer, screenwriter, actor, romantic and playwright. Unfortunately there are no reports of how these two famous people manifest themselves. The third ghost to have been seen is that of the former theatre manager, Charles Morton.

Camden Town, NW1: Old Mother Red Cap Inn

We are indebted to Samuel Palmer who, in his *History of St Pancras*, relays the story of Mother Red Cap of Camden Town. Jinney Bingham was the daughter of a Kentish Town brick maker and a Scottish peddler. She accompanied her mother and father around the country but on her 16th birthday she fell in with a man called Gypsy George Coulter. By all accounts he was a rogue and they used to steal sheep together. After having purloined some sheep from Holloway, Gypsy George had a spell in Newgate Prison, was found guilty at the Old Bailey and was duly hanged at Tyburn. Shortly after this Jinney took up with a man called Darby who inexplicably disappeared. At about the same time her parents were called before the courts on a charge of witchcraft. They had conspired to kill a girl and they were both hanged. Once her parents were dead and Darby had gone, Jinney lived with a man called Pitcher, but he too was destined to die. The remains of his body were found crouched in an oven. Jinney was tried for the murder but during witness testimony it was claimed and believed that Pitcher would hide himself in the oven to escape Jinney's wicked tongue.

For a time Jinney's life was difficult, but presently a homeless fugitive knocked on her door and persuaded her to give him lodgings. After a while he died, and although it was believed that he was poisoned, there was no evidence to incriminate Jinney. Rumours held that the man had left a great deal of money. Jinney continued to live on her own. The locals believed that she was a witch and she was often consulted as a fortune-teller and healer. On one occasion, when a treatment went wrong, she was attacked by a mob of locals. By this time she had taken to wearing a red cap on her head. She was described as having a heavy, broad nose, thick eyebrows and sunken eyes. She had a wrinkled forehead, a wide mouth and a sullen look on her face. She habitually wore a striped blanket around her shoulders that had patches all over it that people believed were bats. On the day of her death it was widely reported that witnesses had seen the Devil himself go into her house to claim her soul. Her body had been found in the morning beside the fireplace. Before her was a teapot of herbs that had been fashioned into a potion. When one of the people gave a cat some of the liquid, its hair fell out within two hours and it soon died.

As for Mother Red Cap, her body was so stiff that the funeral director had to resort to breaking her bones to get her into the coffin. It is believed that the Old Mother Red Cap Inn that was built on the site of her cottage still sees signs of her restless and tormented spirit.

Carthusian Street, EC1: The Sutton Arms

The ghost of a red-haired man who has been christened 'Charley' has been seen in various parts of this bow-fronted public house. On one occasion in 1997 a friend of the landlord saw the red-haired man standing behind her while she was combing her hair. As she turned to face him he disappeared. On another occasion two female customers were having lunch in the main bar when the apparition materialised between them. They claim that 'Charley' smiled and then vanished. Unfortunately it is not known who 'Charley' is and, apart from the colour of his hair, his only other distinguishing feature is the fact that he is wearing an old-fashioned costume.

Catford, SE6: Lesness Abbey

Lesness Abbey, a 12th-century building, was inhabited by Augustinian monks from 1178 until 1524 when Cardinal Wolsey dissolved the abbey and it was pulled down. The foundations that can now be seen on the site were excavated during the 20th century. The ghostly figure that has been seen, possibly that of a monk, may have been disturbed by the excavations.

Charing Cross Road, WC2: The Garrick Theatre

Arthur Bourchier managed this late 19th-century theatre for the first 15 years of the 20th century. His ghost seems to be quite active in several parts of the theatre. He has been seen backstage, on the 'Phantom Staircase' and, in more recent years, in the upper levels of the theatre.

Charing Cross underground station : Davenports Magic Shop

Staff at the shop, which is housed in a relatively new subway building, have reported 'feeling' the presence of a male spirit. These feelings are most prominent in the stock room area of the shop, and several of the witnesses feel uncomfortable about entering this section alone.

Charlton, SE7: Charlton House

In 1680 Sir William Ducie sold the Charlton estate to Sir William Langhorne. Langhorne was a wealthy merchant who died at the age of 85 in 1714. Despite two marriages, the second of which was to a 17-year-old girl, when he was in his eighties, he failed to produce a son and heir. As a consequence, his apparition haunts this house, which was designed by Inigo Jones. He seems to be a particularly troublesome spirit and even in death seems to wish to produce an heir. On one occasion his ghost was accused of raping a girl.

There is another apparition in this house with an equally unpleasant story to tell. Following damage to the house renovation work was undertaken that revealed a horrible secret in a chimneybreast in the north wing. Carefully placed on a ledge inside the chimney, partially preserved by the heat and smoke of countless fires, was the body of a baby. This may be a link to the ghost of a servant seen holding a baby in various parts of the house.

Cheam, Surrey: Century Cinema

Many years ago, during the building of the cinema, one of the workmen vanished without a trace. His lunch bag was found hanging near the stage area and his wages were never collected. There is no indication of why he disappeared or what happened to him. Many people believe that the haunting must relate to him and that his body lies somewhere in the vicinity. Strange, shuffling footsteps have been heard in the stage area, and this was confirmed by three local newspapermen who decided to stand vigil there one night.

Chelsea, SW3: Cadogan Hotel

The ghost of the famous actress Lillie Langtry haunts the dining rooms of this hotel, in what used to be her living area when she lived here. She was the mistress of Edward VII when he was Prince of Wales and she is said to appear at times when the hotel is quiet. She appears to be shy and retiring, causing no problems for the residents or staff at the hotel.

Chelsea, SW3: Cheyne Walk

In Tudor times, the area where Cheyne Walk now stands was part of a royal estate. The ghost of a bear harks back to the cruel days of bear-baiting. The phantom animal was seen in the garden of one of the houses in Cheyne Walk as recently as the mid-1920s. It is believed that there was a bear pit here until the 16th century. The bear has also been sighted at the Tower of London.

The novelist George Eliot (Mary Ann Evans) died in No.6 Cheyne Walk in 1880. A friend of hers, Katharine Macquoid, also a writer, saw Eliot standing at the bottom of her bed one morning and was puzzled. She found out later that her friend had died that night.

The pub called the King's Head and Eight Bells is situated on Cheyne Walk and is haunted by an unseen ghost that has caused the landlord and his wife several problems.

Apparently the ghost becomes particularly active when a new member of staff is taken on, particularly if that person is female. Witnesses have had the feeling that someone has brushed past them, particularly on the stairs of the building, and objects have been inexplicably moved around. The ghost's other activities include turning on gas cylinders in the cellar and switching off the central heating system.

Chelsea, SW3: Elystan Street

In the 1820s a policeman was lynched on this street. The haunting relates to this, but involves not only the apparition of the murdered man, but also that of the baying crowd that killed him. The house outside which the apparitions appear was a former tomb-maker's yard, although it had to be rebuilt after World War Two when it was flattened by German bombs.

Chelsea, SW3: Glebe Place

One of the houses along this road is haunted by a horse, an apparition which relates to the original house on the site, which was demolished during the 1920s. Apparently, this original house was built in the style of a French château and used to be occupied by Dr Phene. Dr Phene and his bride were due to live in the house together, but she tragically died just before the ceremony was to take place. A distraught Dr Phene became an eccentric, and it is reported that his bride's wedding breakfast remained laid on his table for years after her death. When his horse died Dr Phene had the animal buried within the grounds of the house so that he could see its grave. Subsequently, after Dr Phene himself died, many witnesses reported seeing the apparition of a man riding a horse in the immediate area. The horse's skeleton was discovered during renovation work on the building.

Chelsea, SW3: Lower Richmond Road

The Ranelagh pleasure gardens were a place of public amusement in Chelsea between 1742 and 1803. They were named after the Earl of Ranelagh, an earlier owner of the land. One of the ladies of the time was sitting with her lover, Paul, in the grounds when a jealous rival stabbed the man in the back. Two apparitions appear as a result of this murder; firstly, the murderer himself is seen to ride his horse up the drive and into the road, and secondly, the apparition of the broken-hearted woman slowly and mournfully walks along. She cries, wrings her hands and calls the name of her lover.

Chelsea, SW3: Markham Square

A pig-faced lady named Tamakin Skinker, born in 1618 in Germany, once lived in Windsor. Her body was perfectly normal, but her nose resembled that of a pig and her eyes were small and swine-like. Apparently she could speak no English and communicated in either Dutch or French. At one point £40,000 was offered to any man who would marry her, according to Elliott O'Donnell's pamphlet *A Certain Relation of the Hog-faced Gentlewoman*. At some point she lived in Chelsea, but her movements are confused, as her other residences include Blackfriars and Covent Garden. The actor William Barrett and his wife encountered the ghost of this unfortunate woman, which caused the lady to faint, whereupon the pig-faced apparition disappeared. It seems that she originally haunted a house in Blackfriars but her ghost has moved to Markham Square.

Chiswick, W4: Chiswick House, Burlington Lane

Richard Boyle, the Earl of Burlington, designed this house in 1725, in the Palladian style that he introduced in London. The house was the final resting place of two former Prime Ministers. Charles Fox died here in 1806, followed by George Canning in 1827. The building was also the site of a lunatic asylum for several years in the late 19th century. However, it is the ghost of 'one of the mad cooks' that is said to be present in Chiswick House, and it is manifested through the smell of bacon and eggs. No food has been cooked in the house for years, and the cooking smell comes from the area where the kitchens were once situated. Those working at the house have also reported a feeling of being watched during the evening. One witness, while looking in a mirror in one of the bedrooms, reported seeing the reflection of a female apparition standing behind her. When she turned to investigate she could see nothing. Others claim to have sensed a female presence in the bedroom.

The grounds of the house boast yet another manifestation, that of a dark, shadowy figure that lurks and moves through the shrubs and trees.

Chiswick, W4: Chiswick Warehouse, Heathfield Terrace

This building is now a block of flats, but the second floor of this former furniture warehouse had an unknown presence that frightened the staff of the building. They refused to work alone on this floor and often complained that the rooms at this level had an unnatural chill and strange shapes presented themselves to lone workers. One man witnessed the apparition of an old man walking past him and disappearing through a locked door, while others felt a phantom finger poke them in the back while they worked.

Chiswick, W4: Esmond Road

Severe poltergeist activity at one of the council houses on this road caused the son of the occupier in 1956 to be sent away for a time. Apparently, according to psychic experts, the 13-year-old boy, called David, was the cause of the strange and dangerous activities of the unseen manifestation. Despite the fact that no apparition was ever seen, the family went through the bizarre experience of having pennies and other coins thrown at them, often being directly hit. The poltergeist then progressed to throwing razor blades and spanners and this was when the authorities were called in to investigate. After some research, by the police as well as by psychic experts, it was decided that the poltergeist's main target was David. He was sent to live with relatives in another location and, fortunately for everybody, the poltergeist did not follow him. The activities ceased at Esmond Road as soon as David had left the building and they did not occur again even when David returned home to live.

Chiswick, W4: Police Station, Linden Gardens

Formerly a fire station, this police station is built on the site of a building called Linden House and is haunted by Mrs Abercrombie, the mother-in-law of Thomas Wainwright. Thomas Wainwright was born at Linden House and after service in the army married Eliza Ward. The two settled in London, where he became established as an artist. His mother-in-law and sister-in-law became his models. By 1822 he was very short of money and tried to forge signatures in order to obtain money that had been left to him in trust by his grandfather. However, his uncle died and he naturally and legally inherited Linden House, although the family fortune was not as large as he had hoped. At about the same time his mother-in-law and sister-in-law moved into Linden House with them and very shortly afterwards, his wife's mother, Mrs Abercrombie, became very ill with convulsions and died of a stomach complaint. Within a week his sister-in-law had died of the same thing. Wainwright was arrested and sent to Newgate Prison but there was not enough evidence for him to be tried for the murders. He was, however, found guilty of fraud and transported to Australia. Mrs Abercrombie haunted the building when it was a fire station, usually in the basement area. Witnesses reported hearing brisk footsteps during the night, but when anybody turned on the light the sounds would stop abruptly. She has also appeared as a spectral figure on the third floor of the current police station.

Chiswick, W4: St Nicholas with St Mary Magdalene Church

Despite the fact that this church has a very interesting history, records are not held before the time of Oliver Cromwell as it is thought that his soldiers burned the paperwork in order to keep themselves warm. The two hauntings in the churchyard are in fact directly related to Oliver Cromwell. His two daughters, Mary Fauconburg and Frances Rich, are buried in a vault in the churchyard and their manifestations present themselves as white-clad figures. They appear at dawn and disappear into the walls of the church itself. It is said that after Cromwell died, when his body was exhumed and beheaded at Tyburn, his daughter Mary bribed one of the guards at the place of execution for her father's head. She then took it to Chiswick and buried it in the family vault where she knew her sister and herself would finally be put to rest. This story was partially confirmed in 1882 when an inquisitive vicar opened the Cromwell family vault and discovered a third coffin. Concerned that this might bring unwanted public interest to the vault, he rapidly sealed it up without ever opening the coffin to see whether the rumours were true or not. This explanation for the resting place of Cromwell's head is contradicted by the fact that a Dr Wilkinson presented the head to Sidney Sussex College, Cambridge, in 1960. Although there is a plaque at the college commemorating the interment of the head, its actual resting place is unknown. Since 1960 several witnesses have claimed to have seen a pale yellow head without ears, or a large pale blue eye in the south wing of Chapel Court. These hauntings are said to be related to Oliver Cromwell.

Chiswick, W4: The Black Lion, Black Lion Lane

In one of the rooms of this pub, the Long Room, witnesses have reported seeing the apparition of a little girl. The child is said to skip around the room, to be very pretty and to look and be dressed like Alice in Wonderland. When witnesses enter the room and attempt to approach the little girl she is said to disappear.

Chiswick, W4: The Old Burlington pub, Church Street

Dick Turpin, the famous highwayman, is said to have frequented this house, a former Tudor-period pub. However, it is not his ghost that haunts the present-day building, but someone that the locals choose to call Percy. It is not known who

Percy is or why he has chosen this location for his haunting, but he has been seen wearing a black hat and billowing cloak, staring out of one of the windows of the upper floors.

Chiswick, W4: The Tabard Inn

This building has been a public house since the end of the 19th century and an unknown old woman haunts it. Her apparition regularly sits at one of the tables in the bar. She is dressed all in black and her facial expression gives the impression that she is whistling to herself, although no sound has ever been heard by any of the witnesses of her manifestation.

Chiswick, W4: Walpole House, Chiswick Mall

Built in the 17th century, this house in Chiswick Mall was the home of one of Britain's most beautiful women, Barbara Villiers, Duchess of Cleveland and mistress of King Charles II. She apparently bore the king several children but was later usurped by Louise de Kéroualle (the future Duchess of Portsmouth). In her old age Barbara Villiers became haggard and obese. She spent hours pacing up and down in front of her drawing-room window, praying for her beauty to be restored to her. She died in 1709 from dropsy. Her ghost has been seen many times at the house, accompanied by the sounds of the tapping of her high-heeled shoes. She wrings her hands in despair as she stands in front of the window and the sound of her shoes has been heard pacing up and down her former drawing-room.

Clapham Common, SW4: The Plough Inn

The apparition of a ghost known as Sarah has been seen in the form of a white lady, with her long black hair hanging loosely over her shoulders. The pub was built in the early part of the 19th century, but a sealed room was discovered only recently. The top floor had three outside windows, but only two doors leading to rooms from the inside. Strangely, the window of the third room was sometimes open, despite the fact that it was bricked up from the inside. The landlord and staff have often seen Sarah, but there are no clues as to why she has chosen to haunt this pub. In 1970 a landlord was sacked for spending too much time trying to find out Sarah's identity.

Clarence House, The Mall, SW1

The house was built in 1825 for King William IV who was, at the time, the Duke of Clarence. Although it is now the home of the Queen Mother, it was once the headquarters of the Foreign Relations Department of the British Red Cross Society. The building is haunted by the third son of Queen Victoria, Arthur, Duke of Connaught, who lived there from 1900 until his death in 1942. One particular

witness, Sonia Marsh, was working alone in the building on a Saturday afternoon in October. She got the distinct impression that someone was watching her. As she turned around she saw a strange, triangular, grey smoking apparition moving toward her, giving her the impression that it was part of a body moving up and down as if walking. Understandably she fled but on the following Monday morning when she recounted her tale to a work colleague, she was told that there had been numerous sightings of the ghost of the old Duke of Connaught by several other members of staff.

(top right) Steps running down from Cleopatra's Needle.

(top left) The steps up from the river at Cleopatra's Needle.

Cleopatra's Needle, WC2

A strange, silent apparition, thought to be the ghost of one of the many people who have chosen this spot to commit suicide, has been seen on numerous occasions. The ghost is described as being male, tall and naked. Witnesses have seen him jump from the parapet beside the needle and hit the water but create no splash. Other witnesses have clearly heard strange laughing and moans in the vicinity. Cleopatra's Needle, on the Victoria Embankment, was sculpted over 3,000 years ago and is reported to have been cursed by the legendary Egyptian queen.

Clerkenwell, WC1: Dougherty Street

Charles Dickens lived in Dougherty Street between 1837 and 1839 with his wife, Catherine. It was during the time he was living here that *The Pickwick Papers* became popular and successful. His ghost has been seen walking in and out of the house and, on some occasions, standing in the street. He has been described by witnesses as being a short, well-dressed man in a dark suit and coat, with a stovepipe hat on his head. Dickens saved the house from demolition in 1923 by buying the freehold of the property. The house now houses the Dickens House Museum.

Cleopatra's Needle is said to be cursed by the Egyptian queen.

Clerkenwell, WC1: The House of Detention

Although this building was almost completely demolished in 1890, after housing prisoners for some 300 years, it is now a museum. Hauntings have been reported on a regular basis since the museum was opened in 1983 and it is believed that some areas of the former prison have never been entered since they were sealed up during demolition. The hauntings include a woman who appears to be frantically searching for something and the cries of a sobbing child. There have also been reports of the unexplained feeling of an inhospitable presence in some areas of the building. Unidentified footsteps have been heard, as have the sounds of doors being bolted. The museum's sound system has turned on of its own accord and strange and unpleasant smells have been experienced in certain areas.

Colindale, NW9

A vicious and unpleasant apparition is said to haunt the area of the Hyde. It is the ghost of a haymaker who was pitchforked to death by one of his colleagues. The apparition now seems to take pleasure in attempting to use his own pitchfork on unfortunate victims that may encounter him. There is also some talk of a strange manifestation of a multi-coloured donkey. It is said to have the ability to temporarily blind witnesses who look at it.

Connaught Road, E16: The Connaught Arms

The top floor of the pub is haunted by the ghost of an old woman who is said to have been mad and committed suicide. She was the elderly aunt of the current landlord and after she died, the room in which she slept could not be kept tidy and no one would sleep in there. At 6am one morning, a barman discovered the manifestation of the old woman with an evil look in her eyes. Her mouth was twisted into an evil shape. The two dogs that the man had with him were terrified.

Cornhill, EC3: St Michael's Church

In the early 16th century a group of campanologists were ringing the bells during a particularly violent thunderstorm. Suddenly an ugly misshapen figure floated in through one of the windows and gravitated toward the other window. The group of people slumped into unconsciousness, and when they came to the stonework was scarred as if some huge beast had clawed at it. These marks are known as 'the Devil's claw marks'.

Covent Garden underground station, where the actor William Terris has been sighted.

Covent Garden, WC2: Covent Garden underground station

William Terris, who was murdered outside the stage door of the Adelphi Theatre in

King Street, Covent Garden, where Lord Mohun's lover witnessed his apparition in 1674.

December 1897, has been seen many times at Covent Garden underground station. He used the station while travelling between the theatre and his home in Putney and often visited the baker's shop that used to stand here. He wears his white gloves, an old-fashioned grey suit and a Homburg hat. It was impossible to track down any commuters that claim to have seen him, but various members of the station staff, particularly near the staff restroom, have witnessed his apparition.

During the 1950s one member of staff, Jack Hayden, saw the ghost on some 40 separate occasions. Some of his colleagues also saw the apparition, and a séance was held at which the ghost was positively identified as being that of the late William Terris.

Covent Garden, WC2: King Street

In 1674, the eldest son of Lord Mohun was involved in an argument with Prince Griffin. They agreed that a duel should be fought between them, with swords, on horseback at Chelsea Fields. At 10am on the morning of the duel, Mohun passed a place called Ebury Farm. He was waylaid by a party of men, who picked a fight with him and shot him dead. At exactly the same time, his lover was lying in bed in their King Street home. Young Mohun opened the curtains of her bed and looked in at her in complete silence. He then left, although she pleaded with him to stay.

Cranford Park, nr Hounslow, Essex: Cranford House

Two apparitions haunt what little remains of this former home of the Berkeleys. One is the apparition of a man who has been seen in the area of the stables, and the other is a female ghost that was seen in the kitchen before that portion of the house was demolished. The entire area is said to be rather forbidding, but this may be due to the fact that it is often shrouded in fog from the river.

Cripplegate, EC2: St Giles Cripplegate Church

A monument stands in the church to the memory of the wife of a 19th-century shoemaker. Apparently the man buried his wife in her wedding clothes, wearing her wedding ring. A thief enticed the churchwarden to open the coffin and, finding it impossible to remove the wedding ring, began to cut off her finger. As he did so the woman sat up in the coffin and, amazingly, stole the lantern from the thief, walked home and lived for several years after that. The thief may have been the sexton of the church. Not surprisingly the 'dead' wife returned to her home and knocked on the door. When the maidservant opened the door she screamed and slammed the door in her mistress's face, presumably believing she had seen a ghost. Presently the husband opened the door, embraced his wife and over the next few years the couple had four additional children.

Despite this apparent case of catalepsy the poor woman was known from then on as the 'Cripplegate ghost'.

Crouch Hill, N8: Mountview Theatre School and Art Centre

The apparition of a little girl, perhaps around 12 years old, dressed in a late 19th-century pinafore smock, has been seen several times. It is believed that she was either the victim or the murderer involved in a scandal that led to the school being closed down in the 1890s. On a couple of occasions the apparition has been known to hold the hand of someone standing on the stage late at night.

Croydon, Surrey: Addiscombe Station, Lower Addiscombe Road

After the Addiscombe to Elmers End railway line was closed in 1997 to make way for Croydon's new tramlink system, developers and conservationists embarked on a long battle regarding the site. The Southeastern & Chatham Railway Preservation Society intended to use the buildings as a steam engine museum. For many years a ghost that would start and stop trains and open doors had haunted the station sheds and the station building itself. It was believed that redeveloping the site would simply antagonise the spirit. Unfortunately, the developers got their own way and the bulldozers came in to demolish the station, which will become the site of 65 homes and a park. It was proposed that one of the carriage sheds could be preserved in order to provide a home for the restless railway spirit.

Croydon, Surrey: Biggin Hill

A ghostly spitfire from World War Two haunts the airfield. It is believed that it harps back to a fatal crash that occurred during the Battle of Britain. On some occasions witnesses have heard only the sound of the engine, but in other instances people have seen the aircraft flying above the airfield or coming into land. It seems that the key date is 19 January.

Croydon, Surrey: Croydon Airport/Roundshaw housing estate

The ghost of a Dutch pilot, killed shortly after the airport was opened, has been seen still wearing his flying kit. His presence was said to foretell the imminent closure of the airport by fog. The unfortunate pilot crashed just after take off in thick fog and on several occasions has actually warned other pilots that the conditions will soon be very similar to those he encountered when he died.

In 1940 a perfume factory on the site was hit in one of the first air raids on the city. Sixty people were also killed when a bomb hit an air raid shelter. Many witnesses have heard wartime communal singing emanating from the area.

In January 1947 12 passengers died after their aircraft crashed and burst into flames during a snowstorm. Three of the dead were nuns, and they can be seen walking around the airfield. They were Mother Superior Eugène Jousselot, and Sisters Helen Lester and Eugène Martin of the Congrégation des Filles de la Sagesse, who were all travelling on the Spencer Airways Dakota bound for Salisbury. It collided with an aircraft flying in from Czechoslovakia. The ghostly nuns are usually seen on the road. However, in 1976 one of the nuns manifested herself in the sitting room of one of the houses on the nearby Roundshaw housing estate. The occupier was so distressed at seeing the figure that she moved out of her house.

Community singing has also been heard emanating from the boiler house that serves the Roundshaw estate. This building was a canteen during World War Two but was destroyed by a bomb.

Those travelling early in the morning have seen a ghostly motorcyclist driving silently along the main road. He is said to turn into the boiler house and then disappear.

Croydon, Surrey: The Old Palace, Old Palace Road

The history of this site dates back at least as far as the Domesday Book of 1086. Lanfranc, the archbishop of Canterbury, who held the post during the reigns of William I and William II, owned the manor at Croydon. At the end of the 12th century the archbishops of Canterbury also acquired Lambeth Palace, but the Old Palace remained a favoured summer retreat and retirement home. During the archbishops' use of the building the following royal visitors stayed as honoured guests: Henry II (1229), Henry III (1264), Edward I (1274), Edward II (1326 and 1329), Henry VII (1498), Henry VIII (1509), Mary I (1566) and Elizabeth I (1559). It is believed that the archbishops of Canterbury stopped using the building in around 1758. Later, in the 19th century, it became a bleaching factory, but the Duke of Newcastle subsequently bought the building in 1887 and gave it to the Sisters of the Church, who ran it as a school for orphans. It is this connection that probably explains the nature of the haunting in the building. A woman has often been seen walking around, wringing her hands in despair. She appears to be wearing late 19th or early 20th-century clothing and is believed to be the mother of a child that was taken here when it was an orphanage. The building is now known as the Old Palace School and some 800 girls are taught there.

Crystal Palace, SE19

An unfortunate plate-layer, working on the track in the tunnel that runs from Crystal Palace to Gypsy Hill, was decapitated in an accident and can still be seen wandering through the tunnel.

There is also said to be a train bricked up in an abandoned tunnel. This may be the source of a haunting experienced by several witnesses in 1978, which immediately followed the discovery of the train after a girl had fallen down a lift shaft. The official explanation behind the train is that it was an experimental vehicle that proved to be something of a failure and was consequently bricked up and forgotten for many years.

Dean Street, W1: Royalty Theatre

The Royalty Theatre stood in Dean Street, but has now been demolished. Built in 1840, it was on the site of a Queen Anne period house. The White Lady that haunted the theatre was said to date from this period and was often seen walking down the stairway leading to the vestibule. Once she arrived there, she would let out a piercing scream, and then vanish. In the basement, to add credence to the story, the skeleton of a murdered 18th-century woman was found.

Another ghost was that of a gypsy girl dressed in green and scarlet, who walked down a non-existent staircase and through the offices that now stand on the site. Again, she was a murder victim, and when the theatre was built, her body was found encased in plaster of Paris.

The ghost of a Grey Lady, thought to have been Fanny Kelly, has also been seen

69
DEAN ST.

the gargoyle club
7439 1100

here. She was an actress, who became manager of the theatre when it was built. After she committed suicide, she was seen sitting in her favourite box on a number of occasions. Fanny Kelly was the founder of Miss Kelly's Theatre and Dramatic School in 1840, which later became The Old Royalty Theatre. She died in 1882. In 1934 her ghost was seen after many such appearances watching a rehearsal.

Dean Street has a ghost that brings with her the smell of gardenias.

Dean Street, W1: The Gargoyle Club

Nell Gwynne was said to have lived here while she worked as a barmaid in Drury Lane. The haunting may not be that of Nell, but perhaps the same ghosts that haunted the Royalty Theatre next door. The apparition has been described as being a grey, shadowy figure. She wears a high-waisted dress and a large flowered hat, and walks across the floor before disappearing into an old lift shaft. Whenever she appears, she is accompanied by an overpowering smell of gardenias. A tall cowled and shrouded figure has been seen outside the club, but disappears when approached.

Docklands, E14: The Gun Inn, Coldharbour

This was a favoured meeting place of Horatio Nelson and Lady Emma Hamilton. Nelson's ghost has been seen here on a number of occasions.

Back in 1970 the author Frank Smythe created a ghost story with the help of some of his friends. He wanted to discover whether people would believe his story and write about it. Smythe created the ghost of an old vicar that had white hair and walked with a stick. He claimed that he was the ghost of a man who owned a house on the banks of the Thames who lured sailors into his house and murdered them, dumping their bodies in the river. The tale was taken as fact and many other witnesses came forward to support his original story. However, it is possible that not all of these witnesses were being deliberately deceitful. Some investigators point to this kind of story as evidence of hallucinations and other psychological reasons for seeing ghosts.

Downing Street, SW1: No.10

No.10 Downing Street has been haunted for many years. The apparition, dressed in Regency-style clothes, has been seen in various parts of the house, both inside and out. Workmen reported that they had seen a misty-white old-fashioned figure, crossing the garden to the rear of the building. Some witnesses feel that the manifestation is that of a former Prime Minister. It is said that the manifestation only visits the property when Britain faces a crisis.

Drury Lane, WC2: Theatre Royal

A 'Man in Grey' haunts the theatre and is said to be the ghost of a slim man,

thought to be an Arnold Woodruff, who was very handsome with a powerful chin. Descriptions seem to date him to the 1770s as he is dressed in a grey riding cloak, white wig and riding boots and the tip of his sword can be seen from under his cloak. He also wears a three-cornered hat. The ghost had an actress girlfriend, but the theatre manager wanted her attentions and stabbed the man and walled up the body in a passageway near the stage. In 1848, a small room was discovered, in which was the skeleton of a young man wearing the remnants of a riding coat, with a knife sticking out of his ribs. The ghost has been seen by literally hundreds of people, including Sir Harry Secombe and his dresser during a performance of *The Four Musketeers*. In fact, on one occasion 50 people saw him at the same time. The 'Man in Grey' is regarded as a sign of a successful production, so an offer from an exorcist to deal with the ghost was turned down.

The Green Room at the theatre was the scene of a vicious killing in 1735. Charles Macklin murdered another actor, Thomas Hallam, after an argument over a wig. Macklin's ghost has been seen near the orchestra pit, usually in the early evening. Macklin was charged with manslaughter but apparently got off on a technicality. It is said that he died aged 107.

Other ghosts include the comedian Dan Leno, who committed suicide in 1904 at the age of 44. He has been seen by many actors, including Stanley Lupino, another clown, in his favourite dressing room. Others have heard the sound of Leno's feet practising his famous clog dance and sightings of him have also been reported at Collin's Music Hall, where he often worked.

The figure of a white-faced, painted clown has been seen sitting in one of the boxes, and this is thought to be the apparition of the clown, Joe Grimaldi, who has also been seen at Sadler's Wells. During the 1948 run of *Oklahoma!* several witnesses claim to have seen a royal entourage on the stage. It is believed that this was the ghost of Charles II, who apparently had a great love for Drury Lane as it was opened during his reign. During the same run of *Oklahoma!* an American actress called Betty-Jo Jones claimed that she felt hands pushing her to a different part of the stage and that they continued to guide her during her performance. Doreen Duke, who was auditioning for a part in *The King and I*, claims to have felt the same invisible hands that Betty-Jo Jones had felt during her try-out for a part. It is believed that this is another manifestation of Joe Grimaldi.

Charles Kean, the 19th-century actor, is also said to haunt the theatre and is described as wearing old-fashioned clothes. He sits in one of the rows of seats and is apparently only visible during a performance. When the theatre lights go up he disappears.

Dulwich, SE23: Honor Oak Park, Honor Oak Road

In September 1948, two witnesses saw the figure of a woman dancing around the trees. They described her as being about 20 years old and wearing a black coat with a white apron underneath. The ground was uneven and covered in twigs and fallen leaves, yet the woman made no sound as she danced. The apparition has been seen on several other occasions, but no one seems to know who she is.

Ealing, W5: Amherst Lodge

Ghostly footsteps have been heard at Amherst Lodge, perhaps those of a nun that has been seen in the building. One particular witness saw a nun bending over a patient, only to see her slowly vanish. At one stage the building was used as an orphanage run by a group of nuns.

Ealing, W5: Ealing Common

An old-fashioned blue or black coach, perhaps from the 18th century, has been seen crossing the common, pulled by two mottled grey horses. The sighting is accompanied by the sound of coach wheels turning and horses' hooves skittering along. As the manifestation approaches the Uxbridge Road, the apparition is said to vanish. This was a route taken by coaches during the 1700s, and the apparition has appeared, complete with driver, on a number of occasions, the most recent being in 1976.

Ealing, W5: Montpelier Place

It is thought that 21 people died in No.16, a Victorian house, which claimed its first victim in 1887. Anne Hinchfield was just 12 when she jumped 70ft to her doom from the tower of the building. In 1934 a double tragedy occurred when a nursemaid jumped to her death holding a young child in her arms. The house was described as having an evil atmosphere and a strange smell every 28 days. It is believed that some malevolent spirit convinced the 'suicides' that they were walking into the garden and not to their deaths. Thankfully, the house was demolished just after World War Two. However, visitors since the war have also reported feeling hands helping them walk up the steps of the tower and a strange feeling on reaching the top. One witness stated that he felt an almost overwhelming need to jump from the tower. The occupants of the flats that currently stand on this site have reported hearing unusual noises, and there have been inexplicable gas leaks in the building.

Eaton Place, SW1

On 22 June 1893, Lady Tryon was giving a party at Eaton Place and the cream of Victorian society was in attendance. Suddenly, a haggard-faced figure in full naval uniform entered the room. It was Admiral Sir George Tryon, and at the moment of his appearance, his body was lying in the wreckage of his flagship, HMS *Victoria*, at the bottom of the Mediterranean. Sir George's squadron was taking part in manoeuvres off the coast of Tripoli. He ordered that both columns turn toward one another. His ship collided with HMS *Camperdown* and sank with a great loss of life. His apparition was seen just after the ship had settled beneath the waves.

Edmonton, N9: Edmonton Church

Several witnesses have seen the apparition of a phantom white dog at the church. It is apparently harmless provided it is ignored. The ghost of a labourer killed by a bullock has also been seen. The labourer died at a place known as Wire Hall, now demolished. This building was the site of a murder that left the place so badly haunted that it was bricked up for 50 years before being pulled down. A cook working at the hall murdered another member of the staff, leaving an indelible mark of the deed on the building.

Embankment, SW3

One of the arches on the Embankment is haunted by what is thought to be the ghost of a murdered Victorian prostitute. Jenny was strangled by one of her customers and the sounds of the strangulation can still be heard today in the form of her choked screams and the sound of her heels beating against the ground, presumably trying to attract the attention of some passer by.

Enfield, EN1

In late August 1977, a semi-detached council house became the centre of intense poltergeist activity focussed on the family of Peggy Harper and her daughters Janet and Rose. On the first night the children complained to their mother that their beds were 'jolting up and down and going all funny'. The activity stopped as soon as their mother entered their bedroom. The next night, shortly after 9.30pm, the children complained that they could hear a strange, shuffling noise, like somebody crossing the floor in their slippers. As soon as their mother turned off the lights it started again. A little later there were loud knocks on the wall and Peggy actually saw a chest of drawers moving across the floor. As soon as she pushed it back it started to move again. She tried to push it back once more but it would not move. By this time Peggy had realised that the children were not making the stories up and that it was time to get them out of the house. With the children safely next door the police were called and they, too, heard the knocking sounds and saw a chair moving across the floor. One of the officers actually chronicled what he had seen in a statement.

The following day some of the children's toys whizzed around the house, and were hot to the touch when they were picked up off the floor. This continued for three days until Peggy called in a local vicar and a medium. She also contacted the

Daily Mirror, which sent a reporter and a photographer to the house. They sat, waiting for something to happen, for some time, until they finally gave up and headed for their car. The children's toy bricks and marbles then began to whizz around the house again, and as the photographer tried to take a picture of what was happening, a plastic brick hit him on the forehead. When the photograph was later developed there was an inexplicable blank space in the picture. The *Daily Mail* also sent a senior reporter, George Fallows, to investigate the phenomena, and at his suggestion Peggy called the Society for Psychical Research, which sent Maurice Grosse to investigate. By the time he arrived on 5 September the phenomena appeared to have abated. However, on 8 September, while staying at the house, the investigator heard a noise in Janet's bedroom and discovered that a bedside chair had been thrown across the room and was lying on its side, despite the fact that Janet was sound asleep. The chair was seen moving again an hour later, and this time the investigator managed to photograph the incident.

This was not the end of the phenomena. The house was plagued by mechanical and electrical faults and failures. When BBC Radio reporters took tape recorders into the house they discovered that their recordings would often be erased or that some of the metal components in the recorders were bent. Tape decks would also disappear for several hours at a time. Grosse was still investigating the house and was joined by Guy Lyon Playfair, the writer, and together they studied the phenomena in the house for two years. In Playfair's book about the house, *This House is Haunted*, he wrote:

> The knocking on the walls and floors became an almost nightly occurrence, furniture slid across the floor and was thrown down the stairs, drawers were wrenched out of dressing tables. Toys and other objects would fly across the room, bedclothes would be pulled off, water was found in mysterious puddles on the floors, there were outbreaks of fire followed by their inexplicable extinguishing.

The children both claimed that they had felt some invisible force pull them out of their beds and that on other occasions curtains had wrapped themselves around their necks. Peggy supported these allegations. Most unnervingly, the situation reached a crescendo when Janet lapsed into a coma or trance-like state. She would speak in a husky, male voice and claim that she was Bill. The voice also claimed to be several other people and would often swear. Bill claimed to be a previous tenant in the house and said that he had died there. Initially local doctors and psychiatrists believed that Janet was developing a second personality, but this was later discounted. Grosse was determined to follow up the 'Bill' line of enquiry and began to ask what he now believed to be a poltergeist a series of questions, in the course of which he discovered that the spirit of Bill had lived in the house for 53 years. Meanwhile, Janet was sent to the Maudsley Hospital for examination, but no abnormalities were found. Interestingly, the poltergeist activity ceased while she was away from the house.

The head of physics at Birkbeck College, Professor Hasted, investigated some of the physical forms of the haunting. Two more researchers from the Society for Psychical Research became convinced that Janet and her sister Rose were manufacturing the manifestations, and they did catch the pair pretending to talk in strange voices and throwing things around the room. To this day we do not know whether the phenomenon was genuine or not. After a while the phenomena ceased altogether. The case, whether genuine or not, does display some of the characteristics often attributed to similar hauntings. The presence of children reaching puberty has often been linked with poltergeist activity.

Enfield, EN5: Barnet Road

A murder that took place in 1832 is said to be the cause of the haunting that now takes place along this stretch of road. Mr Danby was the person murdered and it is his apparition that causes animals to become terrified. Horses have been said to bolt and gallop at breakneck speed when they have encountered the ghost. The man is tall, with a deathly white face and a gaping wound in his neck. He always stops beside a certain gate along the roadside and then slowly disappears.

Enfield, EN1: Bell Lane

The phantom stagecoach called the *Enfield Flyer* has often been seen travelling at speed some five or six feet above the road surface. The *Enfield Flyer* is a black coach, with two female passengers wearing large hats on board. It seems to have a connection with the nearby River Lea. In the past, the ground near the river was higher (accounting for the 'floating' of the coach), and a coach resembling the manifestation crashed off the road and into the flooded river, presumably killing all the passengers. The ghostly coach was last seen in 1961.

Enfield, EN1: Crown and Horses

This pub has been the site of at least two sudden deaths, one in 1816 and one in 1832. On one occasion witnesses saw the apparition of an old woman pass one of the windows. Another time the ghost was seen inside the pub, despite the fact that the building was closed and locked. The sounds of banging doors and footsteps have been heard. Unfortunately it is not known who the apparition is, but it is assumed that she had something to do with one of the two deaths.

Enfield, EN4: Hadley Road

In 1622 a witch was blamed for much of the suffering that went on in and around this area of London, particularly illnesses that occurred. It is now known that plague was in fact responsible. However, the woman in question was executed and her apparition still frequents the area. She has been described as 'a stooped and gnarled old hag, dressed in black and hobbling along slowly and painfully'.

Enfield, EN1: Oak Avenue

One of the houses at the top of the hill on this avenue is said to have a ghostly presence in one of its bedrooms. The presence is said to make constant low, sighing noises, which increase as time goes on. Occupants of the room also claim to feel a presence whenever they are within the confines of the house itself. It is not known who this presence is or why it has chosen to inhabit this house.

Enfield, EN1: Royal British Legion Headquarters

The apparition of a man wearing black trousers, a white shirt and a black tie has been seen standing in a corner of the cellar. When approached by a barman on one occasion the apparition vanished. Since then several other staff and customers have seen the ghost and heard footsteps walking across the floor of the upstairs bar. There also seems to be poltergeist activity here, as glasses are often found smashed. Before becoming the property of the British Legion, this building was a fire station. It is believed that a fireman was crushed to death by his own tender in the building, and that a woman had an accident trying out the fireman's pole and fatally injured herself.

Enfield Chase, EN2: Camelot Moat

Geoffrey de Mandeville, Earl of Essex, seems to have been a wholly unpleasant individual who built up his fortune by preying on the very people that he had been charged by the king to protect. When the king discovered that he was a bandit and extortioner he had him outlawed. The Earl fled to the Fenlands, where he continued his activities until his death. He was killed at Mildenhall in Suffolk in 1144, but his ghost has been seen here and at many other places at around Christmas every fifth year. He haunts Trent Park, Cockfosters, South Mimms, Monken Hadley and East Barnet, where he owned land. Witnesses describe him as being a fully armed knight, with a red cloak and a red plume in his helmet. It is thought that the figure is guarding treasure that he buried in a well. Attempts have been made to retrieve the treasure from the well, but each time an attempt is made the chains break and the chest falls back into the well.

Farringdon underground station, EC1

A milliner's shop used to occupy part of the site that now houses Farringdon underground station. According to stories told in the area, the owner of the shop and her daughter murdered a 13-year-old girl named Anne Naylor near here in 1758. Anne manifests herself in the form of loud, heart-rending screams that have caused witnesses to nickname her the 'Screaming Spectre'. Her screams have been heard in several parts of the station.

Fleet Street, EC4

During the 17th century a man called Thomas Cox was a Hackney carriage driver in London. On Hallowe'en night in 1684, he dropped off a passenger close to Fleet Street. Cox called at a local pub, then got back into his carriage and started to make his way toward the top of the street. A man carrying a rolled-up parchment flagged him down and Cox stopped the carriage. The man asked him to go to Lower Church Yard and climbed into the carriage. Unusually, Cox's horses were unwilling to move and began to behave in an unusual manner, forcing Cox to ask his passenger to alight from the carriage while he sorted the animals out. The man did as he was asked. Eventually, the total lack of co-operation from the horses forced Cox to tell the man that he could not take him to Lower Church Yard. The man offered Cox an outstretched hand, but it contained no money so Cox assumed the man was offering his hand in a farewell gesture. He went to take hold of the hand, but as he did so there was nothing there and his passenger had turned into 'a great black thing in the form of a Bear with great flaming Eyes which lay by the Wall side and made up to him'. Cox lashed at the image of the bear with his whip and it vanished in a flash of fire and sparks. It is reported that Thomas Cox managed to recover from the incident sufficiently to tell of his encounter, but was left permanently paralysed.

Forest Hill, SE23: Horniman Museum

A ghostly couple have been seen on the terrace, clad in evening dress, dancing on the brick balcony beside the greenhouse. From the description they appear to date from the 1920s. The man has heavily greased hair and the woman is wearing a red dress. They are not accompanied by music, and after their dance they disappear into the trees.

Another dancing figure, but this time a lone one, has also been reported in the area of the museum. The manifestation is of a young girl, dancing in an area known as One Tree Hill. Nothing is known about the origins of this manifestation.

Garlick Hill, EC4: St James's Church

Built by Richard Rothing in 1326, this church was rebuilt by Sir Christopher Wren in 1682 in the aftermath of the Great Fire of London. It contains a mummified

body thought to be at least 500 years old, whose ghost has been seen on several occasions. It was found in 1839 when excavations took place and has acquired the name 'Jimmy Garlick'. He may be one of the lord mayors of London buried in the church. The graves of six former lord mayors of London are can be found in the cemetery of this church. Jimmy's glass coffin bore the inscription 'Stop stranger, stop as you pass by. As you are now, so once was I. As I am now, you soon will be, so pray prepare to follow me' and contained Jimmy's mummified remains. It seems that Jimmy's spirit was disturbed in 1942 when an unexploded bomb fell through the roof of the church. Since then different witnesses in various sections of the church have seen him on a number of occasions. The apparition is described as being tall, swathed in white and with a face like a dried-out corpse.

Alternative explanations identify the corpse as that of a Roman general, Richard Rothing or Henry Fitzailwyn, who died in 1212. The ghost may even be that of Dick Whittington. It is highly unlikely whether we will ever know for sure, as all records prior to 1666 were lost in the Great Fire of London.

A ghostly cat also appears at the church of St James, both inside the building and in the cemetery.

Gower Street, NW1

Gower Street is haunted by the figure of a man who is said to have had his head swathed in bandages. He is dressed in clothes of the pre-World War Two period and

Garlick Hill, said to be haunted by 'Jimmy Garlick'.

St James's Church, Garlick Hill, houses the remains of former lord mayors of London.

said to be enveloped in his own light. It is thought that the ghost is that of a man who stayed at a boarding house in Gower Street and used a local teashop. He is thought to have died in 1936.

Gower Street, NW1: University College

Built in 1828, this building houses the preserved body of Jeremy Bentham, co-founder of the college. The skeleton is dressed in Bentham's clothes. His head is made of wax, although his actual skull is kept elsewhere on the university campus. Bentham's will specified that he was to be dissected in the presence of friends and that his remains were to be preserved and kept on the college grounds at all times. Once a year they were to be present at board meetings of the university governors. Bentham's ghost has been seen several times in the corridors, tapping with his favourite stick and wearing his white gloves. It is thought that his apparition, and the tapping of his stick on the glass front of the case which houses his remains, is an attempt to force the college officials to give his body over for a proper burial.

Gower Street, NW1: University College Hospital

The ghost of Lizzie Church, an early 20th-century nurse, is said to haunt the hospital. It is said that she accidentally gave an overdose of morphine to her fiancé,

University College Hospital.

a patient who died as a result. Overcome by remorse, she also died, but many witnesses have seen her apparition dressed in an old-fashioned uniform, supervising morphine injections to help ensure that no further mistakes are made.

Green Park, SW1

Known by locals as 'The Tree of Evil', one of the trees in the park is even said to frighten the birds away. Those wishing to commit suicide by hanging themselves have used the tree on a number of occasions. Witnesses have reported the sound of an evil chuckle emanating from the tree, as well as a dark, shadowy figure standing next to it. Apparently the figure disappears instantly if the witness attempts to move closer to the tree.

Jeremy Bentham inside his glass case.

Greenwich, SE10: *Cutty Sark*

Although there are no reports that the *Cutty Sark* is haunted in its current dry-dock position, there is an interesting tale relating to the times when the vessel sailed the seas. Built in 1869, the *Cutty Sark* was adorned with a figurehead that was placed aboard the ship in order to protect its sailors from the risks associated with sailing the high seas. Often the sailors on board would recount their tales of seeing phantom ships and those afraid of the stories would gather beneath the figurehead to gain protection. Shortly after joining the crew of the *Cutty Sark*, one particular young sailor placed a model of the figurehead in a glass bottle, much to the dismay of his colleagues who considered this to be inviting bad luck. Within days a severe storm caused the waves to crash around the *Cutty Sark*. During the storm the sailors saw, looming toward them, an enormous ship. They all feared for their lives. Seeking the protection of the figurehead, they gathered beneath it in their traditional manner. The *Cutty Sark* all but capsized and the waves continued to lash at the ship for the duration of the storm. Once the winds and waves had ceased the sailors looked for the ship that had come so close to their bows but the vessel had totally vanished. Apparently at the exact second that the vessel had disappeared, the young sailor had thrown his 'figurehead in a bottle' into the waves.

Greenwich, SE10: Royal Naval College and Queen Anne's House

Elizabeth I was born at Greenwich Palace, on the site of which the Royal Naval College now stands. She lived there happily for many years and it would seem that she is reluctant to leave the building as her ghost remains. She has been seen walking around several different parts of the building and the extensive grounds. Witnesses report that she looks exactly as one would expect, wearing an ornate dress, her red wig and a crown.

A photograph of the Tulip Staircase in Queen Anne's House revealed the figure of a cowled monk climbing the stairs, accompanied by a less-clear figure. A ring could clearly be seen on the hand of one of the figures. There was once an abbot's house at Greenwich, so perhaps the cowled figures were monks from that period.

In 1756 Admiral Byng was defeated in a sea battle against the French while attempting to relieve the British garrison at Minorca, and he was brought back to stand trial by court-martial at Greenwich. He stayed in Queen Anne's house until he was executed. Door handles move on their own and doors have been thrown open. Footsteps have also been heard in the corridors, leading people to believe that Byng's spirit is attempting to make the injustice of his death known.

Greenwich, SE10: St John's Library, St John's Park

This building was formerly the vicarage of St John's Church. The Revd Marshall

Queen's Walk, Green Park, site of a tree known as the 'Tree of Evil'.

became the vicar in 1874. His daughter, Elsie, was destined to become a missionary in China and it is her untimely death at the hands of brigands thousands of miles from home that is the source of the haunting of this building. She left for China in 1892, arrived there safely and soon began work at a remote mission station where she had a reputation for her patience and cheerful nature. On 1 August 1895 Chinese bandits attacked the mission station and murdered everyone before ransacking the buildings. Although it is not known exactly where Elsie was buried, it is certain that her ghostly spirit made the return trip to her Greenwich home. Many of the staff, despite the fact that they have never seen her, have felt her cold presence brush past them, and they have been the butt of many of her practical jokes. It is said that she moves things around and gets particular pleasure from switching lights on and off unexpectedly.

Greenwich, SE10: Ship and Billet Inn, Trafalgar Road

Lord John Angerstein used to frequent this public house regularly, and presumably cannot bear to be parted from his favourite drinking place. His ghost can be seen dressed in a black velvet coat, breeches, stockings and silver-buckled shoes during the month of November. His phantom coach and four horses collect him from the Ship and Billet Inn on the stroke of 6 o'clock.

Greenwich, SE10: Trafalgar Tavern, Park Row

Charles Dickens immortalised this 19th-century public house in *Little Dorrit*, but he was not the only famous writer to frequent the tavern. Wilkie Collins and William Makepeace Thackeray also visited it on a regular basis. Back in 1977 the then bar manager claimed to have seen a man dressed in Victorian clothing sitting beside the piano upstairs. A previous landlady was convinced that the building was haunted, but was content enough with the presence of her unearthly lodger that she would greet him each morning. Currently many of the staff and customers claim to feel a chill in the air, the feeling of a presence and occasionally those that live in the pub have seen a figure walking quickly through one of the upstairs rooms. Some staff have claimed that crates of beer have been moved around in the cellar while they have been working.

Greenwich Park, SE10: Crooms Hill Gate, Chesterfield Walk

This perplexing and fascinating tale probably dates back over 1,500 years. The area was believed to have been a women's cemetery in the fifth or sixth century. It appears that the original investigations into the causes of several manifestations of women in procession date back to 1789, when a Revd Douglas established the fact that a graveyard had been here. What is particularly interesting about the manifestations is that they are blissfully unaware of the fact that the ground has been raised considerably since their burial, so they are seen only from the knees up. Back in 1934 a description was made of the procession appearing to a passer-by. A woman was walking her dog beside Crooms Hill Gate when her canine companion stopped and began to growl. At first she could not see why it was behaving in this way, but presently she saw a procession of women. They all seemed to have red hair and were dressed in crude, woollen clothing. The group were carrying a roughly hewn coffin on their shoulders. She could not see their feet and it looked as if they were walking through the earth. As they approached the gate itself the whole group disappeared. Her description matches those given by other witnesses. When visiting the site you can see the indistinct outlines of burial mounds or barrows near the gate. It is believed that the manifestations have a definite connection with these ancient tombs.

Guy's Hospital, SE1: St Thomas Street

Built in the 1720s, the hospital is haunted by a ghostly ward sister. She has been seen to put her arms around patients that are in need of reassurance about their condition.

Another manifestation is present, which is heard and not seen. Three members of staff were talking outside a ward in which an elderly female patient lay dying. They heard footsteps walking toward the ward, through the doors and down toward the old lady's bed. The doctor and the two nurses could also hear the creaking of new boots. The sounds came back and then disappeared. When they checked the old lady, she had died.

Hackney Road, E2: Nag's Head

After a series of strange sounds and odd happenings at this public house, one of the cellar men encountered the probable cause of the problems. The witness described the ghost as appearing to be an old woman in a long, Victorian dress with a grey shawl wrapped around her shoulders. After a séance the spirit of the old woman seems calmer than she was in the past.

Hallam Street, W1

During the 1930s Sherard Cowper-Coles moved into one of the flats on this street. He is famous for developing the method of producing a protective zinc coating on iron and steel products in 1904. Because his wife had not yet joined him at his new flat, he set up a tripod to take some photographs to send to her. When he had the film developed he was very puzzled to find that in the photographs of his living room, an unknown man was sitting in his pink and white chintz armchair. The apparition was only partially visible and seemed transparent. Cowper-Coles decided to take more photographs and each time there was a different apparition present when they were developed. Eventually he had quite a collection, including warriors, one of Wellington's soldiers, women and one that his brother later identified as being their childhood nursemaid. Apparently Sherard could not remember the lady in question but his elder brother could.

Ham House, nr Richmond, Surrey

Built in 1610, the house is haunted by the ghost of Lady Lauderdale, who lived there in the 1670s. She is said to have been a particularly unpleasant individual with, appropriately, an equally unpleasant husband. Her ghost has been seen on numerous occasions walking around the building tapping the floorboards with a cane. Some witnesses also report hearing the faint strains of *Greensleeves*. Whether the haunting and the music are linked is unknown. One sighting of particular note was by a six-year-old girl, who was awoken by the sounds of fingernails scratching at the wall. The ghost turned to look at the child, who screamed in terror. When the wall was investigated, marks were found, beneath which were hidden documents that proved that Lady Lauderdale had murdered her previous husband, Count Dysart.

Hammersmith, W6: Beavor Lane

One of the buildings in this lane was built by Samuel Beavor during the 18th century and was the former home of Sir William Richmond and his family. The 'grey lady', with evil, staring eyes, was often seen by members of the Richmond household, and was accompanied by some poltergeist activity. Windows were repeatedly shaken in the middle of the night and doors were inexplicably opened and closed. Strange human-like noises were also heard in the form of sobbing and sighing. Apparently there are two possible explanations for the presence of the manifestation of the grey lady. One is that she was a nun who had an illegitimate child. To cover up the scandal she murdered the baby and buried it. The other possible explanation is that a gang of forgers once lived in or near the property. One night an old woman caught them carrying out their illegal practices. They murdered her and sewed her into a sack that they then threw into the River Thames.

The Richmond family also encountered a group they called the 'Roystering Beavorites'. This ghostly group of partygoers was never seen but was heard in the small hours of the night. Loud voices and the sound of doors slamming were heard, just as if a party were coming to an end and the guests were leaving the premises.

Hampstead, NW3: Church Row

A rather unsavoury crime during the 19th century involved the death of a child in Church Row. A housemaid left in charge of a child murdered it and took the body out of the house in a carpet-bag. The red-haired apparition of the murderess can often be seen leaving the house in a furtive manner.

Hampstead, NW3: East Heath Road

This area of Hampstead is haunted by a figure that is so lifelike that he has frightened many people who only realised that he was an apparition when he disappeared into thin air. The man is described as having a toothless grin and wearing a brown jacket. He appears from nowhere and follows those walking along this stretch of road. Then, just as abruptly, he vanishes back into the air.

Hampstead, NW3: Holly Bush Inn, Holly Mount

This pub is built on the site of stables that used to be attached to the nearby house, owned by the painter George Romney. Two ghosts, one female and one unseen, haunt this pub. The unseen one is in the form of a hand that is said to pat the back of the pianist that performs in the pub, as if congratulating him on his performance. The female ghost takes the form of a waitress and attends the tables in the dining area of the pub. This often causes great confusion and frustration as the pub operates a bar food-ordering service, not a waitress service.

Hampstead, NW3: Keats House, Keats Grove

The ghost of the poet John Keats has been seen at the front of his former home. Keats lodged in the house with his friend, Charles Armitage Brown, for two years, during which time he became engaged to Fanny Brawne. At the age of 24, ill health from tuberculosis forced him to move to Rome, where he died a year later.

A taxi-driver, believing he had witnessed a publicity stunt for the Keats House Museum, saw the ghost of Keats standing outside the house. He returned the following day and was told the house was closed for renovations. When he explained that the previous day he had seen a man dressed in 19th-century costume, one of the officials took him into the house and showed him a portrait of Keats hanging on one of the walls. It was the same man the driver had seen the day before and he was wearing the same clothes.

Hampstead, NW3: Spaniards Inn

Mounted on Black Bess, the ghost of the infamous highwayman Dick Turpin is seen around the Vale of Heath. Turpin's spirit will gallop toward you and, at the last minute, vanish. Several witnesses near the public house have heard hoof beats. Turpin used to lodge here during time spent in London, although he lived for most of his adult life in York, where he was hanged at York Tyburn on 7 April 1739. The inn itself was built in around 1585 and was originally named after either the Spanish ambassador to King James I, who may have lived there, or after a Spanish landlord by the name of Frances Porrero. An alternative story says that Turpin was actually born here on 21 September 1705. It is certainly the case that his father was the landlord of the inn during the 18th century.

At the nearby Turpin's Restaurant, guests dining have seen the ghost of a strangled girl, apparently murdered in the 1700s, on several occasions.

Hampstead, NW3: The Flask Tavern, Flask Walk

The ghost of a 19th-century landlord called Monty tries to keep a close eye on the activities of the current landlord and staff of this pub. He makes it very obvious if he disapproves of any developments by moving tables around and switching the light on and off. He would appear to prefer the pub to remain as it was in his day.

Hampstead, NW3: The Priory

One of the daughters of the original builder of the house, known later as The Priory, haunts the property. Apparently her father was a somewhat eccentric character, who at some stage had one of his two married daughters buried within the walls of the house.

Hampstead, NW3: William IV

The manifestation of a girl in a white shroud, with long, plaited hair, can be seen peering mournfully in through the windows of the pub. It is said that she committed suicide in the dentist's surgery that was once located opposite.

A female apparition, thought to be that of a former occupant of the building before it was a pub, also haunts the pub itself. Her husband murdered her and her body was bricked up in the walls. The victim of this murder is said to present herself in the form of noises, such as the rattling of windows and the slamming of doors, in the middle of the night.

Hampstead Heath, NW3

Apparently a highwayman was killed on the Heath at some stage in the past and it is said that a stone marks the spot. The stone has been heard to whistle on occasions and has now become known as the Whistling Stone.

Hampton Court Palace, East Molesey, Surrey

There are numerous ghosts at this historical site, all connected to famous individuals associated with this place. Cardinal Wolsey, who actually built the palace, was seen at a performance held there in 1966.

Catherine Howard also haunts the building. After Henry VIII's discovery of her infidelity, she begged him to forgive her and spent many hours in the chapel praying for forgiveness. She was reported to have been physically held down on the execution block on 13 February 1542. As a result, witnesses have heard her fists banging on the door of the chapel and her screams. She has been seen fleeing down the Long Gallery. It is said that during the 19th century the gallery had to be closed down because of her activities. She has also been seen walking the gardens.

Jane Seymour appears as a white lady walking through the Silver Stick Gallery. She died of an infection caught in childbirth after providing Henry with a son and heir, the future Edward VI. She is seen on the anniversary of Edward's birth, 12 October.

The apparition of Mrs Sibell Penn, who died in 1562 of smallpox and was buried in the old church, has also been seen. She was King Edward VI's nurse until he died aged 16 in 1553. She did not begin to haunt the building until her tomb was moved in 1821. She is responsible for the noise of a ghostly spinning wheel, which emanates from a wall in the south-west wing. Sibell Penn has also been seen at her former home, in Penn Place, Hampton.

Toward the end of the last century, two skeletons were discovered in a shallow grave under a door, following a number of disturbances at night.

During World War One, the policeman on duty saw two men and eight women, all phantoms, by the front gate. He could hear the sound of rustling dresses before they all melted into thin air.

Hampton Court Palace, East Molesey, Surrey: Old Court House

There are two ghosts here. The first is an eight-year-old boy, dressed as a 17th-century page, with long hair.

More significant is Christopher Wren, the well-known architect responsible for the design of the South and East Ranges of Hampton Court Palace between 1689 and 1694. Wren is said to appear on 26 February, the anniversary of his death.

Haymarket, SW1: Her Majesty's Theatre

The actor John Baldwin Buckstone was the manager of the theatre in 1853–1878. He haunts his favourite dressing room and witnesses report seeing him enter the room, cross to a certain cupboard, rummage through it and then walk out through the door again. His apparition wears a long, black frock coat. His voice has also been heard rehearsing lines. The actress Margaret Rutherford was one of those who claimed to have seen the apparition, along with Dame Flora Robson and the actor Donald Sinden. On one occasion a member of the cast performing at the theatre saw the apparition sitting in an armchair in his dressing room. He quickly locked

Her Majesty's Theatre, Haymarket, where several actors and actresses have witnessed apparitions.

the door and called the fire brigade. However, when they arrived the room was empty, although it is reported that two of the firemen in attendance saw the man's face reflected in the mirror of the dressing room. The appearance of the apparition usually signifies a long run of the show.

Heathrow Airport, Hounslow, Middlesex: Runway 1

On 2 March 1948, 21 people died when a DC3 aircraft crashed and caught fire. It is believed that the ghost of one of these passengers now walks on Runway 1. In 1970 radar picked up someone walking on the runway. Three police cars and a fire engine were sent to the site and directed to the exact spot. When they arrived they could see nothing. The operator could see the vehicles and the rogue blip and continually gave the police instructions as to where the figure was. As they turned around, they were told that they had actually driven through the figure. On this occasion the apparition chose to be invisible, but on other occasions he has actually been seen. He is described as being a tall man wearing a bowler hat and a pair of twill cavalry trousers. Apparently, shortly after the crash, some of the rescue workers were asked by a man fitting this description if they had found his briefcase.

Highgate, N6/N19: Highgate Cemetery

Several ghosts can be seen in this cemetery, one of the most ornate and strangely forbidding in the country. 'Inhabitants' include Dante Gabriel Rossetti and Charles Dickens. Rosetti, the famous pre-Raphaelite painter and poet, married his favourite model, a woman of outstanding beauty, by the name of Elizabeth Siddal. Tragically she died in 1862, aged only 29. Rossetti placed a manuscript of poems in her coffin when she was buried in Highgate Cemetery. Shortly after her death Rossetti's career went into gradual decline, but his agent, Charles August Howell, who also represented Swinburne and Ruskin, persuaded Rossetti to disinter the coffin and retrieve the poems therein. Rossetti was not present when the body was exhumed, but witnesses reported that Elizabeth's hair had grown and was as beautiful as it had been when she was alive. Rossetti had gone to Scotland, where he began to drink a lethal mixture of whisky and chloral. Subsequently the poems were published in a volume called *The Book from the Grave*. Rossetti died soon after publication, and in 1890 Howell also died under unpleasant circumstances. His body was found with a gold coin jammed between clenched teeth and its throat cut. There are unconfirmed reports that Howell's ghost haunts the area near Elizabeth Siddal's grave.

Reports have also been made of the spirit of an unknown mad woman who searches the graves for children that she murdered, and a sad-looking shrouded male figure that simply sits and stares.

Near the main entrance a ghost with bony fingers lies in wait, and the spirit of a man in a black hat can be seen near the cemetery walls at Swain's Lane. During the 1960s it was believed that a vampire was also present in the Swain's Lane area. The 'Highgate Vampire', as he was known, was exorcised by Bishop Sean Manchester and it was thought that the bloodthirsty entity moved to a house in Crouch End.

Highgate, N10: No.10, Muswell Hill Road

This house used to be occupied by the famous actor Peter Sellers and his mother, Peg. Apparently the two were inseparable and Sellers used to seek his mother's guidance and advice regularly. When she died, it would appear that her spirit continued to have these conversations, because Sellers would make changes to plans, upset his directors and change the location or date of filming as a result of advice that his ghostly mother had given him.

Highgate, N6/N19: Pond Square

In March 1626, Sir Francis Bacon, viscount of St Albans, was being driven through Pond Square in his coach. It was snowing and the pond was frozen. He had the coachman stop and buy a chicken, which he then ordered to be killed. Bacon stuffed snow into the bird and created the first frozen chicken. However, as a result of the experiment, Bacon caught a chill and died of bronchitis at the home of Lord Arundel in Highgate on 9 April.

Many witnesses claim to have seen the partially plucked chicken flapping around the square, making a loud and distressing squealing noise. It eventually disappears through a brick wall.

Highgate, N6: Red Cap Lane

Just before Christmas 1790, a nurse was appointed to care for the only son of a local household. The young man was, by all accounts, on the verge of death. When the nurse arrived in 'Hollow Way', she briefly recounted that a highwayman had stopped her carriage in Red Cap Lane. Although the driver and the nurse were shaken by the experience, the highwayman had let them pass as she carried little of value to him.

According to the story, published in the December 1878 edition of *Mother Shipton's Miscellany*, the nurse arrived at the house and was shown into an oak-panelled room, with a large fireplace and curtained bed. The doctor was leaving just as the nurse settled in, and all he told her was that the patient needed silence. The nurse was intrigued to see her patient.

> ...he was not asleep, but lay motionless on his bed, his bright blue eyes glazing fixed upon her, his under-lip fallen, and mouth apart, his cheeks perfectly hollow and his long, white teeth projecting

fearfully from his shrunken lips, while his bony hand, covered with wiry sinews, was stretched upon the bedclothes, and looked more like the claw of a bird than the fingers of a human being.

At around midnight, the nurse heard the patient breathing heavily and saw a veiled woman sitting beside his bed. As the nurse rose, the figure motioned for her to stay seated. The patient continued to convulse and breathe heavily until the nurse closed her eyes for a moment. When she reopened them, the figure was gone and the patient more relaxed.

The scene was repeated the next night, with the nurse becoming increasingly concerned about the appearance of the woman and her effect on the patient. The following night was Christmas Eve and the nurse was determined to see the woman again, as she had never let her enter the room. After some time she reluctantly closed her eyes, only to open them again to see that the visitor was present once more. This time the patient 'gasped and heaved till the noise of his agony made her heart sicken within her; when she drew near the bed his corpse-like features were horribly convulsed and his ghastly eyes straining from their sunken sockets'. She touched him and his body was cold. The nurse thought that the patient was about to die. The visitor had moved away from the bed, but presently returned to it, creating the same effect on the patient. Suddenly the visitor turned and headed for the door, but the nurse intercepted her and attempted to raise her veil to discover who she was, but fainted as she did so. 'As she glanced on the face of the lady, she saw that a lifeless head filled the bonnet, its vacant sockets and ghastly teeth were all that could be seen beneath the folds of the veil'.

The nurse was found lying on the floor in the morning. The patient was dead and one of his hands was across his eyes, while the other still gripped the bedclothes.

That same day, Christmas day, the body of a woman was found on the shore at Queenhithe. The body had been in the water for at least three or four days. Documents in her pocket linked her with the patient. Whether the young man had killed her and her spirit had returned to exact revenge upon him from beyond the grave is a matter for speculation. Obviously, given the countenance of the apparition that the nurse had seen and the probable state of the corpse washed up at Queenhithe, it would have been impossible to make a definite identification.

Highgate, N6: The Flask, West Hill

A female ghost haunts this 18th-century pub, and there are several theories about who she may be. Some believe that she is the apparition of a girl who committed suicide as a result of a failed love affair, while others think she is the spirit of the woman portrayed in a portrait hanging in the pub. The third theory is that she is in some way connected to the bullet that is embedded in one of the walls. In fact, nothing is really known about who she is, although her presence does make itself known to the landlord and staff of the pub. There are sudden drops in temperature when she is around, lights switch themselves on and then off again, and customers have witnessed glasses moving of their own accord, as well as feeling someone blowing on their necks.

Highgate Hill, N6: Beechcroft Way, Elthorne Road

The block of flats situated at the bottom of Highgate Hill was built in 1975 and owned by the GLC. Intense poltergeist activity was experienced during 1978 in one of the flats. Objects were inexplicably moved around the home and some of the tenant's possessions went missing. The occupants of the flat and their neighbours saw the misty shape of a figure. After an exorcism the poltergeist activity quietened down. It is not known what caused the activities or who the misty shaped figure may have been.

Highgate Hill, N6: Ye Olde Gate House

Dating back to 1310, this used to be a favoured stopping point for drovers *en route* to Smithfield. The ghost of an old woman haunts the building, appearing as a black-robed figure. This is the spirit of Mother Marnes, who was murdered, along with her cat, by a robber. The apparition does not appear if children or animals are present, although her manifestation, when it does appear, is said to be terrifying.

Holborn, WC1: The Peacock Theatre, Kingsway

The present building replaced a former theatre in 1960. The former theatre, the London Opera House, became the Stoll Theatre before it was demolished in 1958. Oscar Hammerstein had a mistress who was an actress and built the London Opera House. Apparently this unknown mistress haunted the previous building.

Holland Park, W8/W11: Holland House

Built in 1607 by Sir William Cope, Holland House was once the home of the Royalist Sir William Rich, Earl of Holland. It has now been substantially rebuilt, following its near destruction during the Blitz. Rich was executed at Palace Yard in 1649 during the English Civil War and Oliver Cromwell gave the house to General Fairfax, a Parliamentarian military commander. Rich's ghost haunts the house, and he is often seen in the Gilt Room, holding his head in his hand as he appears from a hidden doorway and walks slowly through the room at midnight. Three spots of blood are said to mark the spot where his manifestation appears, and efforts to remove them have met with failure. He was also seen by a group of students in 1965 while they were in the gardens of the house.

The grounds of the house also boast strange encounters, but this time they are predictions rather than the manifestations of a ghost. All three of Sir William Rich's daughters are reported to have seen visions of themselves shortly before they died unexpectedly. Lady Diana, Lady Isabella and Lady Mary all saw their own mirrored faces as a warning of their approaching deaths.

Holland Park, W8: No.51, Peel Street

The former occupiers of this house, as well as many of their friends and visitors, experienced inexplicable noises here. The sounds of muffled footsteps have been heard on many occasions, as recently as 1961. It is reported that when the house was being constructed two of the workmen on the roof section of the building fell and were killed. It is not known whether the ghostly footsteps are connected with this accident.

Hornsey, N8: Ferrestone Road

On 1 January 1921, the inhabitants of the house on this road, the Frost family, heard a series of explosions that seemed to emanate from either the fire grate or coal buckets. It appears that lumps of coal were exploding and fragments were found in all parts of the house, damaging furniture and smashing ornaments. The Frost family had three children, Gordon, Bertie and Muriel, who saw tea plates rise from the table while they were eating a meal. On another occasion the father stood aghast as he saw one of his sons being lifted into the air along with the chair on which he was seated. This, apparently, reoccurred on a number of occasions. The family were perplexed and initially called in the police. While an inspector was examining a piece of coal it shattered into pieces in his hand and disappeared. The family's local vicar, the Revd A.L. Gardiner, saw a piece of coal move along a shelf and fall to the floor. Dr Herbert Lemerle apparently witnessed a clock vanishing before his eyes. It seems apparent that the phenomena were so terrifying that they helped cause the death of Muriel. She died on 1 April. As to an explanation for these strange occurrences, a public meeting was held on 8 May 1921 that identified the fact that all of the strange phenomena occurred when one of the boys in the family was present. It was believed that the ghost was the boys' aunt. She had died a year before and it is said that one of the boys actually saw her apparition. Gordon suffered a nervous breakdown as a result of the haunting and spent some time in Lewisham hospital.

Hyde Park, W1: The Devil's Elm

Also known as 'Black Sally's Tree', vagrants avoid sleeping under this elm, as they are likely to be found dead in the morning. In the 1920s, a man murdered his wife, known as 'Black Sally', under the tree. It is said that moaning sounds have been heard coming from the spot where her body was found. In all respects, the tree is considered to be evil.

Hyde Park Corner, W1: Apsley House

This house was given by a grateful British public to Arthur Wellesley, the Duke of Wellington, and now houses a museum dedicated to his life and work as a soldier and a politician. During a period of unpopularity in the 1830s he was mobbed by crowds and had iron shutters fixed to the property in order to protect him from missiles being hurled at him from the streets. The ghost of Oliver Cromwell appeared to the Duke of Wellington during this time and the manifestation pointed a finger at the growing number of people objecting outside. Apparently this caused the Duke to give up his battle to oppose the Reform Bill.

Ickenham, nr Uxbridge, Middlesex: Ickenham railway station

The apparition of a middle-aged woman with a red scarf haunts the station. Several years ago the unknown woman was reported to have fallen onto the electrified rails and been killed. Obviously something about the station or the accident is making it impossible for her to rest in peace.

Ilford, Essex: Old Fire Station, Ilford Broadway

Geoffrey Netherwood, a fireman in Victorian times, was obsessed with the supernatural. It is not therefore surprising that after his ceremonial burial, he returned to the station to haunt the building. He was seen by several of his former colleagues and other witnesses have seen him since. He appears in his full uniform, despite the fact that the fire station has moved to Romford.

Isleworth, Middlesex: Osterley Park House

The apparition of a white lady has been seen on many occasions, usually at 4.30pm, standing near the left-hand arch under the main staircase, near the entrance hall. She appears in her fine, flowing gown, stands in position for a few seconds and then moves toward the doorway and vanishes. It is believed that she was a former mistress of the house.

Islington, N1: No.113, Bride's Street

Michael Faraday, who discovered the principle of electro-magnetic induction, was an elder of the Sandemanian sect that once occupied No.113. There is a plate on the floor that marks the position of his pew when it was a chapel. On several occasions Faraday's ghost has been seen walking through the building.

Islington, N1: Old Queen's Head, Essex Road

Although the original building was pulled down in 1829, this site has been a public house since the reign of Elizabeth I. She herself used the public house, the license for which was granted by Sir Walter Raleigh. One of the upper rooms was sealed after child victims of the plague died there in 1665. On the first Sunday of each month, doors inexplicably swing open and then close, and the sound of footsteps coming down the stairs can be heard. Landlords and customers claim to have seen a sad-looking little girl and a woman dressed in Elizabethan costume, accompanied by footsteps and the swish of a dress. It is also said that there is a tunnel from the Queen's Head to Cannonbury Tower, which enabled Elizabeth I to visit her lover, the Earl of Sussex.

Islington, N1: Trinity Church, Liverpool Road

A man called Richard Cloudesley, a benefactor of the parish, died and was buried in the churchyard in 1517. He has become known as the 'Islington Ghost'. Apparently after his burial the ground around his grave began to tremble and swell and 'turned up every side towards the midst of the field'. It became apparent to the witnesses that Richard Cloudesley was not content and that an exorcism was required to quieten his soul. In the dead of night, using torchlight, the exorcism took place and 'the earth did return to its pristine shape'. It is reported that 1,000 masses had to be said before his ghost was laid to rest. In 1813 Richard Cloudesley's grave was opened and his remains were moved.

Islington Green, N1: Collins Music Hall

Sam Collins used to own this music hall and always used seat No.6 in row B. After his death he continued to occupy the same seat even when a performance was not showing on the stage. The cleaners in the hall became used to his presence and carried on working regardless. Other witnesses have seen Collins walk through one of the cellar walls.

The building was demolished in 1963 following a fire, but it was haunted by its founder, a man called Vagg. He opened the theatre in the 1860s. Witnesses saw doors slam shut and felt icy fingers on their faces.

Dan Leno, the celebrated music hall entertainer, was also seen there after his death, sitting in the same seat near the front of the stalls.

K

Kensington, W8: Kensington Palace

Queen Victoria was born here and William III, Queen Anne and George II all died here, but it is George II who has actually been seen in his phantom form. It is believed that George would have preferred to die in Hanover and was awaiting departure, but gale force winds forced him to stay in England. His ashen-faced ghost has been seen many times, looking out of his bedroom window toward the weather vane. Other witnesses have also heard him ask 'When will they come?'

Another sad figure is also said to haunt this palace. George III's daughter, Princess Sophia, gave birth to the illegitimate son of Thomas Garth, one of the king's equerries. After the baby was born Thomas paid little attention to Sophia and she lived a lonely and sad life at the palace, spending a great deal of her time in solitude at the spinning wheel. As Sophia grew older she became blind and was not even able to use the spinning wheel. Her phantom spinning wheel has been seen in her old room at the palace and its monotonous creaking has reverberated around the building on a number of occasions.

Kensington, SW7: Royal Geographical Society, Kensington Gore

Some years ago a telephonist working at the Royal Geographical Society was given a flat in a building opposite the headquarters as part of her employment package. When she and her husband moved into the flat on the first floor they temporarily set up their bedroom in the living room. In the middle of the night she saw what she describes as the figure of a monk standing over her. She described him as being tall and thin with an unpleasant look on his face, wearing what appeared to be a grubby, white canvas gown. He wore a strange, tasselled hat and when he stared at her with vibrant blue eyes and pointed at her with a bony finger she screamed and woke her husband up. The apparition promptly disappeared.

On the second night, afraid of what she might encounter, the telephonist drowsed rather than slept. She claimed that gradually the room changed, with her own furniture disappearing to be replaced by straw strewn all over the floor. In front of her sat a short man, who looked like a jockey, who offered her a date to eat from his fingers. She described him as having a stubby nose and a ruddy complexion. She later learned that horses had been kept on the first floor of the building as a precaution against theft and that these horses had often been fed dates. The Society's librarian also showed her a photograph of a small man holding the reins of a carriage. It was the same man she had witnessed as an apparition.

On the third night, although anxious, she dropped off to sleep. When she woke a different tall man was standing over her. He was wearing canvas boots, grubby blue shorts and a safari-suit jacket. She described his legs as being white with red hairs. He was wearing a blue slouched hat on his head and had a big, bushy red beard. The apparition seemed unaware of her and stared at the wall beyond her before fading away.

Much later, while entertaining her daughter's friends at her flat, the telephonist had to pop out to get some more drinks from the shops. She opened the front door and saw a tall man wearing a black cloak standing just outside. She immediately shut the door in his face. Other witnesses at that time also saw the apparition. Her daughter opened the door and there was nobody there and the door to the street below was locked. The strange events did not seem to be restricted to her own flat.

Some time later, while sitting at her desk, the telephonist felt an uncontrollable urge to pick up her pen and write. Before she realised it she had written, in copperplate handwriting, 'Edmund S. Knight 1882'. Despite checking to see whether this person had any connection with the Royal Society, no trace could be found of him.

On yet another occasion in her flat she heard a rushing sound rather like water and was concerned that there was a leak somewhere. As the sound got more distinct she realised it was not water and that it sounded like something travelling very fast over ice or snow, strange as it was a sunny day. The only connection that she could make was that the Royal Geographical Society houses Captain Scott's sledge.

Kensington, W10: St Mark's Road

First reported in June 1934, a phantom bus has been seen here. That fateful morning the ghostly No.7 bus caused the death of a motorist whose car burst into flames after having swerved off the road to avoid the apparition. Usually at around 1.15am, the driverless coach has sped toward motorists and vanished just before impact. Research has not uncovered any reason why a No.7 bus should haunt the area, as it seems that they have never passed through St Mark's Road.

Kentish Town, N7: Grafton Road

In the early 1980s an antique dealer bought a suit of armour from a house clearance in Hackney. The Spanish armour was in need of some repair, which he dutifully carried out before displaying it in his shop for several months before an Arab customer purchased it. Having concluded the deal the overseas buyer drove off in his Rolls-Royce. The antique dealer, meanwhile, had the suit of armour delivered to the man's London address. Very soon after this the antique dealer began to see the manifestation of a tall and bearded man. He described him as being noble in appearance but with a very sad expression on his face. What was equally perplexing about the haunting was the fact that the figure was only wearing flimsy undergarments. The antique dealer linked the manifestation with the armour and immediately contacted his Arab buyer, only to discover that he had already taken the armour to his home in the Middle East. It is said that the knight, without his armour, still haunts the shop in Grafton Road.

**St James's Theatre,
King Street, is
haunted by three
ghosts.**

Kentish Town, N7: Hilldrop Crescent

Doctor Hawley Harvey Crippen was hanged for the murder of his wife, Cora, in November 1910. He had been having an affair with a young typist named Ethel Le Neve. He was arrested mid-Atlantic, *en route* to America with his mistress. Supernatural interest, however, revolves around some wasteland near to Crippen's home in Hilldrop Crescent. Just before the murder, Crippen spent several nights walking around on the waste ground, perhaps plotting the deed. When the body was found, the head and other parts were never discovered. It is thought that he may have buried them here. Crippen's ghost has been seen walking around the wasteland with a parcel, heading toward a pond. As the manifestation moves away from the water, he no longer has the parcel. Crippen was hanged at Pentonville prison.

Kidbrook, SE9: Kidbrook Lane

In 1871, Edmund Pook was tried and acquitted for the murder of Jane Maria Clouson. Her head had been battered with a hammer. They had been having an affair and Jane was pregnant, but Edmund had no intention of angering his father by marrying the girl. Despite finding the blood-stained hammer, blood on Edmund's clothing and the fact that Jane accused him on her deathbed, he got off. Her ghost appears as a white lady with her face covered in blood. Witnesses have heard her cries for help and groans.

Kingly Court, W1

The apparition of an 18th-century man strolls around this small passageway. It is not known who the man is, but he is often reported to be whistling to himself and stroking his chin as if deep in thought.

Kings Cross station, WC1: East Coast Mainline

During the 19th century one of the steam locomotive drivers reported the fact that he had encountered a ghost when the train was passing through Hatfield. The fireman on board the same train saw nothing. Apparently a man dressed completely in black and with a sad look on his face stepped onto the platform of the train. The driver saw the man place his hand on the train's regulator and he felt compelled to do the same, thus slowing down the train. The fireman questioned the driver as to why he was slowing down when the line ahead was clear. It was not until the train had completely stopped that they both realised the line ahead was blocked by two trucks. Had it not been for the actions of the ghostly apparition the train would have crashed into them.

King Street, SW1: St James's Theatre

St James's Theatre was opened in 1835. Before that it was Nerot's Hotel, and it is

now an office block. Three ghosts haunt the site. The first is a woman dressed in 18th-century clothes, possibly dating back to its time as a hotel. The second ghost is thought to be that of a former dresser, who still helps actors on with their costumes and brushes them down before they appear on stage.

The third ghost is that of Oscar Wilde. A séance was held at the theatre during the 1920s involving two actors and one actress. A phantom hand appeared and took hold of a pen, and when those in attendance asked the phantom hand to identify its owner, the pen wrote that it was Oscar Wilde. This is, presumably, the man's favourite way of making himself known in the spirit world, as he has contacted several such séances by means of writing both witty and sad comments.

Kingsway, WC2: The Ship Tavern, Gate Street

During the 16th century, when Henry VIII was on the throne, Catholics used this pub to carry out illegal mass services. The priest holes in the pub are evidence of these times. While the services were being performed by the priests, the congregation would take it in turns to stand as lookout for Henry's soldiers. If the premises were raided, the priests would hide in the priest holes until it was over. It is believed that the ghost of one of these priests haunts the pub. He is said to be happy but mischievous and although he has never been seen he has made himself known by hiding various items, sometimes for several days at a time, and then returning them to their correct location.

Knightsbridge, SW7: Lowndes Square

Apparently the mother of a former occupier of one of the houses in this square was taken ill with a stroke and her daughter brought her to live in Lowndes Square. Because of the old woman's ill health, the daughter used to sit her mother outside in a wheelchair on sunny days and the old woman would watch the world go by. Unfortunately she would soon tire of this pastime and, because she was unable to talk to anyone as a result of the stroke, she would communicate with passers-by with her facial expressions and they would ring the bell of the house so that her daughter could fetch her back inside. The ghost of the old lady continues to do the same thing. Witnesses have reported seeing the old lady in the wheelchair sitting in the square. She has white hair and continues to pull unpleasant and sometimes quite frightening faces at passers-by.

Knightsbridge, SW7: Montpelier Square

A bizarre story dating back to December 1913 relates to one of the houses on Montpelier Square. Apparently a local vicar was approached by an agitated woman who told him that a man was dying in a house nearby. The sick man was very concerned about the fate of his soul and wished to obtain the counsel of a clergyman. The vicar got into a cab with the woman and was driven to Montpelier Square. He got out of the cab and knocked on the door of the house identified by the woman. The butler answered the door and confirmed that the name that the vicar had been given was, indeed, the name of the master of the house. When the vicar started to explain the story that he had been told the butler told him that his master was in perfect health. An explanation from the woman was not forthcoming, as both she and the cab had mysteriously disappeared. The vicar was perplexed but the master of the house, intrigued by the snippets of conversation that he had heard, joined them on the doorstep. While apologising for the apparently wasted journey, he did tell the vicar that he was thinking of calling him because he was, in fact, concerned about his own soul. After an hours' conversation and confession the master of the house agreed to attend a church service the next day. The clergyman left but never saw the man alive again. Not only did the man not make an appearance at the church, but when the vicar spoke to the butler he was told that the master of the house had died a little while after the vicar had left that previous evening.

To confirm what he had told the vicar the butler took him upstairs and showed him his master's body laid out in the bedroom. It was there that the vicar saw a photograph of the woman who had accosted him the day before. He asked the butler who the woman was. He told him that it was his master's wife, who had been dead for 15 years.

The Grenadier experiences ghostly activity in September.

Knightsbridge, SW1: The Grenadier

Many years ago an officer was caught cheating at cards and was taken into the cellar and flogged. He died as a result of his injuries. Particularly in September, the pub experiences an enormous amount of poltergeist activity and on several occasions a figure has been seen standing beside the beds of those sleeping upstairs. The apparition manifests itself by wandering through the empty rooms of the pub, and one witness has reported seeing and feeling hot smoke rising from an unseen cigarette.

The pub is also said to be haunted by a man who committed suicide by electrocuting himself in the bathroom. It is not known if the figure is the flogged soldier or the suicide victim.

Knightsbridge, SW7: Victoria and Albert Museum

It is not the building itself that is haunted but one of the museum's exhibits. The museum houses the 'Great Bed of Ware', thought to have been made for Henry VIII because of its enormous dimensions. Jonas Fosbrooke made the famous huge and elaborate bed during the 16th century, and the carpenter haunts the bed when he feels that its occupants are not worthy of sleeping in it. He has been known to make their night very uncomfortable, by scratching and pinching them.

The Great Bed of Ware is referred to in Shakespeare and other 16th-century sources. It has become the centrepiece of the rebuilt British Galleries, which opened in November 2001. It is said to have originally measured 18½ feet wide by 12 feet long and could accommodate 68 people. Nowadays it is 10 feet 9 inches square.

Ladbroke Grove, W10: Cambridge Gardens

The phantom bus that operates down St Marks Road in Kensington enters Cambridge Gardens at one o'clock in the morning.

One local garage owner reported having to repair many cars that had been damaged as a result of evasive action taken by their drivers in Cambridge Gardens, a situation that was taken so seriously by the local borough council that they widened the road. It was suggested that the bus could have been a late-night staff bus returning duty crews to their homes after work, but witnesses were adamant that although the bus was fully lit there was no sign of a driver or passengers.

Lambeth, SE1: Lambeth Palace

Anne Boleyn was held here and tried for adultery before her execution in the Tower of London. Her ghost can be seen getting into a boat at the river's edge for her last journey to the Tower. Other witnesses have heard her voice crying and sobbing near the door where Archbishop Cranmer presided over the trial in the undercroft.

Part of the palace that was formerly the Lollards prison has a door that locks and unlocks itself. The prison was used to hold individuals, usually Catholics, who were to be burned at the stake.

Lambeth, SE1: St Thomas's Hospital, Lambeth Palace Road

Originally built in the 13th century and dedicated to Thomas Becket, the hospital is haunted by a grey lady. She is described as being middle-aged and dressed in a grey uniform and she has a look of horror in her eyes. Block 8 is one of the few original Victorian hospital buildings that remains today. The grey lady is seen there, and she is believed to be a harbinger of death. On five occasions between 1956 and 1959, patients who saw the grey lady died within days of the sightings. The apparition can only be seen from the knees up, which tallies with the fact that the floors have been raised by 18 inches. There are three theories as to who the grey lady is.

She may be the ghost of a 19th-century nurse, who committed suicide after accidentally killing a newborn child. Alternatively, she could be the manifestation of a nurse who threw herself from the balcony of the building after being reprimanded by the sister in charge of her ward. The third theory is that the grey lady is the ghost of either a nurse or a female patient who died from smallpox in Block 8.

Those who have witnessed the apparition have also reported the sweet smell of moss or mown grass and a severe drop in temperature.

Langham Place, W1: Broadcasting House

A extravagantly moustachioed, limping man, wearing old-fashioned clothes, was seen on the fourth floor of the building in 1937. He looked so life-like that witnesses took little notice of him until he suddenly disappeared before their very eyes.

The apparition of a ghostly waiter has also been seen, as has a musician who appears to witnesses to have lost his way. If help is offered to him the manifestation nods his head and then vanishes.

Langham Place, W1: The Langham

On several occasions the figure of a bearded butler has been seen limping down the third-floor corridor carrying an empty tray. He disappears into one of the rooms along the corridor.

The figure of another apparition has also disturbed several occupants of room 333, and it is believed that he was a World War One German officer who leaped to his death from the fourth floor.

Several presenters from the BBC have witnessed strange apparitions in The Langham, as some of the floors contain accommodation for those broadcasting either late at night or early in the morning.

James Alexander Gordon, Ray Moore and many of their colleagues have witnessed a fluorescent ball that slowly takes human form and becomes a translucent Victorian man dressed in a cloak and a cravat, who floats above the ground with outstretched arms and big hands.

There have also been reports of the sighting of a young girl dressed in either a blue dress or a nightdress. Some reports claim that this girl was, in fact, the

girlfriend of the butler and that he had killed her either during an argument or in order to rid himself of her.

The Langham Hotel.

Leicester Square, WC2: Albery Theatre

Sir Charles Wyndham was the first manager of the theatre in 1903. The Albery Theatre backs onto a theatre that Wyndham had built in 1899. His ghost is said to present itself at the Albery in the form of a distinguished-looking gentleman with a mass of wavy, grey hair.

He has often been seen in the backstage area of the theatre and has also nodded to actors while they are on the stage.

Lewisham, SE13

Along one of the main streets, mournful voices are heard coming out of the sky in the early hours of the morning. One possible explanation seems to relate to the time when the plague was particularly active in this part of the country, and it may be that the spirits of those buried in mass graves around the edges of the city are still restless here. Another theory is that the ghostly voices relate to a train disaster in 1957.

Lincoln's Inn Fields, WC2

Robert Perceval, a law student and cousin of the assassinated Tory Prime Minister, Spencer Perceval, saw his own ghost before he actually died. He was studying when the apparition presented itself to him and he lunged at it with his sword. As he did so the apparition's cloaked face was revealed to him as his own, but badly wounded. Some time later Robert was attacked and murdered by some of his many enemies in the Strand. Students studying in the area that used to be his chambers at Lincoln's Inn have reported seeing the ghost of Robert complete with his badly wounded face.

A dark, shadowy figure has also been reported in this area late at night. The figure is said to accompany the sounds of pain-wracked screams and mainly presents itself in the centre of the square, where a shelter is situated. It is believed that this apparition could be the result of the many executions that took place at this site. Others were disembowelled or hung, drawn and quartered.

Lincoln's Inn Fields, WC2: Royal College of Surgeons

A man called Forster murdered his wife and child and after he was hanged his body was given to the college for dissection. During the experiments the body quivered and one eye opened. The corpse's right hand was seen to rise and clench. By all accounts the man was still alive. Not only is he said to haunt this building, which was his ultimate place of death, but his body's movements also caused a second death. The beadle, Mr Pass, watched the experiments and died of fright on his way home. He, too, is said to stalk the building.

Lombard Street, EC3

During the 17th century a Mr Youngs owned a property in this street. Apparently an incredibly strong ghost that had a habit of slamming shut large windows haunted it. The ghost was reported to have been witnessed by a number of dignitaries at the time, some of whom became weak and dumb at the sight of it. It is not known who the ghost was representing, but it is believed to have vanished spectacularly into the ground with a clap of thunder, a flash of lightning and a puff of sulphurous mist.

London Bridge, E14: The Horns Public House, Crucifix Lane

Sited under the railway arches, this pub is haunted by the manifestation of an old lady. It is not known who she is, but she is thought to have been murdered nearby. The Horns also used to house the apparition of a young girl searching for her mother, but most people do not believe that the two ghosts are linked in any way.

M4 motorway, leading from Heathrow Airport into London

In autumn 1993 a young woman named Becky was driving into London along the M4. The road was quiet with very little traffic. When she saw someone walking in her direction in the distance in the traffic lane she assumed that their car had broken down and that they were seeking help. That was until she passed the walking woman, who was dressed in black and wearing a type of mackintosh or sou'wester and carrying two bags. She thought the woman looked about 60 years old, and she had a very severe, black haircut and her face was pinched and drawn. The woman did not make any attempt to flag down the driver and did not even appear to notice that a car had passed her at high speed.

About a month later the same witness saw the same apparition again at about the same time of day and in the same place, although the passenger in her car was unaware of the ghost.

Marble Arch, W2: Connaught Place

The former place of execution, Tyburn, used to stand here. In 1678 the gallows were inexplicably ruined during the night and general opinion at the time was that it was done by the hands of evil spirits. It was believed that the ghosts of those hanged there had sought their revenge. One spirit was seen the night before, sitting on one of the crossbeams of the gallows, and apparently the man sat with 'his neck awry' making the sound of a screeching owl.

The Tyburn gallows was actually a three-legged structure called the 'Tyburn Tree'. It had galleries and seats around it that were let out to the massive crowds that always appeared when there was an execution. It is said that the prisoners that were brought from Newgate gaol had already had the noose conveniently tied around their necks.

Mayfair, W1: Hill House, Hill Street

On 24 November 1779, Lord Lyttleton was asleep in his room. He was awoken by a strange fluttering noise. Standing by his bed, he saw the figure of a white lady. He recognised it as one of the Amphlet girls. He had seduced them, deserted them and then they had committed suicide. The spirit told him he would be dead before midnight on the third day after the sighting. When the fateful hour approached, with a slight gasp, he dropped his hands to his side and died in the arms of his valet, aged 35. Lyttleton's ghost appeared to one of his friends, Miles Peter Andrews, just as he died, wearing a dressing gown and standing at the foot of his friend's bed in Dartford. The apparition said 'It is all over with me'. Andrews, not knowing that Lyttleton had died, assumed the man had arrived unexpectedly to stay the night.

Running feet, moans and pistol shots haave been heard in Lansdowne Row, Mayfair.

Deciding to play a practical joke, Andrews threw his slippers at Lyttleton, who promptly disappeared. Andrews got out of his bed, thinking he had offended his friend, and went in search of him but he was nowhere to be found.

Mayfair, W1: Lansdowne Passage

Although this was closed and replaced by Lansdowne Row in the 1930s, it is still a very haunted place. Highwaymen used it as an escape route after holding people up in Piccadilly. Witnesses have suggested that they have heard running feet, moans and the occasional pistol shot.

Mayfair, W1: Sheppey's Restaurant, Shepherd Market

Edward Shepherd built Shepherd Market as a cattle market in 1735, and he built his house in Mayfair on the site of an old fair that had been held there since the 13th century. During the middle of the 18th century the ground floor of the building was converted into a coffee house and was frequented by Boswell and Dr Johnson. In 1860, the house was demolished and a new coffee house was built. The ghost of a highwayman, who had lived at the old coffee house during the 18th century and was hanged at Tyburn, haunts the present restaurant. He has been described as being tall and thin and wearing a black cloak.

Mile End Road, E1/E3: The Drivers' Arms

After drinks began disappearing and heavy objects began inexplicably moving about the pub, the landlady called in a medium. After some research the medium came to the conclusion that the poltergeist activity was being caused by a previous landlord. The Victorian man apparently objected to the fact that women were allowed to frequent the pub and to partake of alcohol.

Mill Hill, SW13: Lawrence Street

In 1963, workmen digging in the grounds of St Joseph's Nursing College discovered the coffin of a nun buried in the 19th century. Shortly after this incident, several witnesses reported seeing a cloaked figure in the street. The apparition disappeared when approached. Others reported hearing hymns being sung in the vicinity. It is interesting to note that Lawrence Street was haunted by a cloaked figure during the 1920s. Perhaps, whatever the connection with the disturbed nun, the apparition has chosen to recommence its hauntings.

Shepherd Market, Mayfair, is haunted by a tall, thin highwayman.

Montague Square, WC1: Blooms Town House

Situated adjoining the grounds of the British Museum, this 18th-century building is haunted by what is believed to be the ghost of a regular visitor to the museum.

St Magnus the Martyr church, Monument, is home to the apparition of Miles Coverdale.

What is most interesting about this haunting is the fact that it occurs in room 1 of the hotel, which is actually an extension added to the back of the building, constructed on what was part of the townhouse's garden. It is for this reason that guests describe the ghost as appearing to be sitting, thinking and relaxing. Presumably the ghost is still under the misapprehension that he is sitting outside in the sunshine. The apparition does not appear to take any particular notice of anyone or anything, but always sits in the same chair. A paranormal investigator made a visit to the hotel on the suggestion of an American guest and formed the opinion that this was not the only ghost resident in the hotel. In fact he described the place as being rather over-run by them. It was his belief that being so close to the British Museum that numerous spirits that had emanated from the exhibits had actually taken root there.

Monument, EC3: St Magnus the Martyr, Fish Street Hill

Sir Christopher Wren built the church in 1676. The manifestation of a black-haired priest, believed to be Miles Coverdale, who produced the first English edition of the Bible in 1535, has been seen, accompanied by a feeling of sadness. A former verger's wife said that she had twice seen the figure of a short, black-haired priest kneeling at the same spot. Miles Coverdale was at one time rector of St Magnus the Martyr before becoming Bishop of Exeter. Other sightings include a silent, kneeling, motionless figure wearing a cassock-like garment but with nothing inside the cowl. The sightings are brief and the apparition disappears as suddenly as it appeared.

Museum Street, WC1: Atlantis Bookshop

Just a short walk from the British Museum, this bookshop specialises in the paranormal and the occult. Its ghost is said not to enter the shop itself, but to rattle the door-handle. The man wears an old-fashioned grey suit and he is thought to be the manifestation of one of the previous owners of the shop that was founded in 1922.

Neasden Lane, NW10: St Mary's Church

The church is Victorian, but still retains a significant part of its former 13th-century structure. The church itself is haunted by the spirit of a priest, accompanied by the smell of incense. He has a tendency to rattle the door handles in the vestry. The grounds of the vicarage are haunted by the figure of a rotund monk in a black habit. He is said to be happy-looking, to enjoy walking around the garden, and he tends to be seen near the site of a well that was once used by the vicarage household.

**Amen Court,
Newgate, is the site
of the former
Newgate Prison.**

Newgate, EC1: Amen Court

In 1783, the new Newgate Prison was built and a system of hanging that dropped the prisoner through the floor of the scaffold was introduced. A new scaffold was built outside the prison so that 12 men could be executed at the same time. Between Newgate and the Old Bailey was a small passageway, completely caged in, called Birdcage Walk (or Dead Man's Walk), which was also the location of the lime pits in which the remains of the executed prisoners were buried. Jack Shepherd, the cat burglar, was hanged in November 1724 after having escaped custody three times. Witnesses have seen a dark shape in Birdcage Walk late at night and have heard the sounds of chains and heavy footfalls. It is believed to be Shepherd's phantom.

The ivy-covered wall at the end of Amen Court has been in place since the court and the former prison were in existence. This section of the wall is believed to be haunted by a particularly unpleasant manifestation known for centuries as the 'Black Dog of Newgate'. The Black Dog is said to have been witnessed gliding up and down the streets and crawling along the top of the wall immediately before an execution was to take place. Apparently one prisoner called Luke Hutton wrote down his opinions about the existence of the Black Dog. It is thought that he believed it to be the ghost of a former prisoner called Scholler, who had been eaten by the other starving prisoners. The act of cannibalism caused the prisoners to imagine that they had seen Scholler at night, in the form of a black dog, patrolling the prison, his jaws open in preparation for his revenge.

The ghost of Amelia Dyer, the 19th century baby-farmer who took in orphaned children, claimed money from the parish to look after them and then disposed of them, has also been seen at Newgate. She was executed on 10 June 1896 and on her journey to the scaffold she is reported to have said to Mr Scott, the chief warder, 'I'll meet you again, some day, sir'. Some time later Mr Scott was sitting in the Keeper's Room when he saw the face of Amelia framed in the grille of the door. Scott leapt up and opened the door but there was nobody outside, although there was a woman's handkerchief lying on the floor. There had been no women prisoners at Newgate for years. Apparently Mr Scott was photographed outside the prison soon afterwards and the face of Amelia appeared on the print once the film had been developed.

Newgate Street, EC1: Greyfriars Churchyard

Greyfriars churchyard lies beside the ruined Christ Church, founded by Franciscan monks in 1228. It was said that no matter how evil one was in life, burial in Greyfriars would offer protection from the devil. Queen Isabella 'the she-wolf of France', wife of Edward II and mother of Edward III, left her husband for Piers Gaveston and absconded to France. She returned with an army, defeated Edward II and then imprisoned and murdered him. She ruled for just four years until she was

The rear wall of Newgate Prison is haunted by the 'Black Dog of Newgate'.

defeated by her own son and held 'in protective custody' for the rest of her life. She is buried in Greyfriars churchyard with her husband's heart on her chest. Her ghostly apparition can be seen at twilight, gliding between the trees and shrubs of the churchyard, still holding Edward II's heart in her hands.

Two other ghosts join Isabella: Elizabeth Barton (the Holy Maid of Kent), who, when arrested and interrogated, confessed that she had feigned her trances and invented the religious visions that she had been famous for. She was executed for high treason at Tyburn in 1534; and Lady Alice Hungerford, who was executed at Tyburn in 1523 for poisoning her husband. They appear together in the churchyard on occasions and have even been seen arguing violently with each other.

Newgate Street, EC4: Viaduct Tavern

Mediums visiting this 19th-century pub have experienced strange phenomena, particularly in the cellar area. A sudden drop in temperature, coupled with an unusual and unexpected feeling of sadness or melancholy has been felt, especially in the right-hand corner of the cellar. It is unknown from where this poltergeist activity emanates, but the landlords and staff at the pub now refer to the spirit as 'Fred'. One landlord found himself locked in the cellar one morning, and all the lights went out, with no apparent cause. When his wife finally rescued him it was apparent that the door had been locked from the inside of the cellar as it was easily opened from the outside, although something had prevented the man from releasing himself. This incident, coupled with other experiences in the cellar, has made many of the staff unwilling to go to the cellars on their own.

New Scotland Yard, Parliament Street, SW1

Once the headquarters of the Metropolitan Police, this building now houses the Black Museum, a collection of gruesome criminal exhibits. When it was being built in 1888, a workman found the mutilated remains of a woman. A search of the area produced a foot and other parts of the body. The head was never found, but a silver crucifix engraved with the name of a convent made the police believe that she may have been a nun. Several officers and civilians have seen the dark figure of a headless nun in the basement of the building, which disappears if approached.

Norwood, SE27: St Joseph's College

In 1864 Daniel Philpot, Mr Prior's senior groom, bet his life savings on one of the stable's horses. Prior was a well-known racehorse breeder and Philpot was convinced that this particular horse had all the winning qualities. Philpot lost his life savings on the horse and hanged himself. His ghost appears every five years in the Oak Room. It is said that he will next appear in 2003.

New Scotland Yard now houses the Metropolitan Police Black Museum.

Notting Hill Gate, W11: Coronet Theatre

The ghost of an actor/manager is said to stalk this theatre, particularly the stairs to the circle. It is believed that the man committed suicide and is probably of the Edwardian era. On the few occasions he has actually been seen, he has been described as being middle-aged and wearing an Edwardian suit. The haunting tends to take the form of an uneasy and oppressive atmosphere in that particular area of the theatre.

There have also been sightings of a female cinema cashier. The theatre has been run as a cinema since 1916. Apparently in Christmas week the unfortunate female was discovered to have been fiddling the receipts from the box office, and when the then manager challenged her she fled to the balcony and committed suicide. The cashier's ghost is most active around the anniversary of her death and her footsteps have been heard on the staircase and her shoes have been seen climbing the stairs. Apparently the apparition was responsible for causing so much chaos during staff meetings that the venue for these was changed to a lower part of the building. She also moved around pots of paint that were stored in a room about to be decorated.

Pall Mall, SW1: The Golden Inn, Angel Court

An unknown and unidentifiable apparition has been witnessed in several areas of this pub on a number of occasions. Numerous witnesses have reported sightings that they describe as 'glimpsing from the corner of their eyes'. When they turn to look at the apparition fully it disappears.

Park Royal, NW10: Central Middlesex Hospital

The ghost of a young girl, said to be the apparition of a youngster who was taken into the hospital for a minor operation but was given the wrong anaesthetic, has been seen here. She died in theatre but has been seen in the ward in which she stayed prior to the operation. She is said to be responsible for strange clinking noises that have been heard in the ward. It is also believed that the lift that takes patients to the surgical ward moves up and down of its own free will. This may, of course, be linked to the same haunting.

Peckham, SE15: Old Tower Cinema

The ghost of a middle-aged man has been seen to walk across the stage about 10ft in the air, then disappear into a bricked-up recess that once held the organ. In 1953, two people working late saw the ghost and refused to enter the building again. It was seen again in 1954 by a group of workmen. A number of other strange events have taken place here, including bags of cement being ripped open and water dripping through the ceiling despite the fact that there was no leak. The most probable explanation is that the building was the site of a chapel in the early part of the 19th century. According to a map dating from around 1819, the ground floor used to be about 10ft higher than it is today.

Peckham Rye, SE15: The King's Arms

The King's Arms is built on the site of a 17th-century pub that was destroyed by a direct hit during the Blitz. The bomb smashed through the pub and exploded in the cellar, which was being used as an air-raid shelter, killing 11 people. Footsteps have been heard, objects moved, dogs are petrified and voices singing wartime songs accompanied by a piano have been heard. A female apparition has been seen, who is thought to be one of the regulars killed on that fateful night.

Pentonville Prison, N7

Strange and unaccountable footsteps, coupled with an unpleasant atmosphere, are said to be related to the suicide of a prisoner here many years ago.

The prison is said to be haunted by the ghosts of several prisoners who were held and executed here, as it was used as a place of hanging almost until capital punishment was abolished in 1964.

Piccadilly, W1

According to Elliott O'Donnell, a writer of ghost stories, 'a great clammy hand' haunts one of the apartments in this area of London. The hand becomes particularly active when there are strangers sleeping in the apartment and it approaches their bed, grabs them by the throat and causes them pain and discomfort that they have described as being like a strangulation.

Some years ago, close to the well-known Fortnum & Mason establishment, a young girl was waiting for a taxi. When one finally arrived it was being vacated by a red-haired woman. The girl was in a hurry and the woman seemed to be taking ages to pay the driver because she was having trouble finding the right change. Losing patience, the girl decided to pay the woman's fare herself and was somewhat annoyed when the woman simply walked off without even bothering to thank her. Expressing this annoyance to the taxi driver, he then told the girl that the woman was an aristocrat called 'Lady C' and that she probably had more money than the pair of them put together. When the girl arrived home she recounted the tale to her mother, who promptly went to fetch a newspaper dated three days earlier, the front page of which stated that Lady C had been killed in a fire.

Piccadilly, W1: Burlington Arcade

During the 1970s a leather goods shop in this area experienced some poltergeist activity. The unseen apparition chose on a number of occasions to take all of the items on shelves in the shop from their set locations and place them in a neat pattern on the floor. This occurred several times over a period of four months until, inexplicably, the activities stopped as abruptly as they had begun.

Piccadilly, W1: Naval and Military Club

Major Henry Braddell, known as Perky, was killed in an air raid in 1941 and has been seen in the Egremont Room of the club. He has been quite easily identified from his uniform and ankle-length greatcoat. There is another ghost in the club

that is somewhat more frightening and dangerous. It often jumps out and scares people. Many years ago a man went into a fit just after visiting the club and died. It is believed that this is his apparition.

Piccadilly, W1: Vine Street Police Station

In the early part of the 20th century, a sergeant committed suicide on the premises by hanging himself in one of the cells. As a result, his ghost haunts the police station in the form of heavy footsteps in the corridors. It is believed that his ghostly hobnailed boots make the sounds. He has also been seen in full uniform, staring into the cell in which he ended his life. In recent years he has been blamed for the rearrangement of documents on desks and the sound of cell doors being opened in the night.

Q

Queen Caroline Street, W6: St Paul's Churchyard

The 'Hammersmith ghost' was first seen in 1805 when it chased a woman through the churchyard. It is described as being a tall, white male phantom, believed to be a suicide victim. In 1855, 50 years after the first haunting, a group of vigilantes staked out the churchyard and lay in wait for the manifestation. Unfortunately, they mistook a man in a white smock for the phantom and shot him. The blunderbuss owner was sentenced to death for the killing, but this was later commuted to one year in prison after the courts took account of the circumstances.

Queen Victoria Street, EC4: St Andrew's Church

The haunting of this church centres around the church bell. The bell, called Gabriel, was hung in the tower in 1937, having previously hung in the belfry at Avenbury, Hertfordshire. The bell apparently rings when a vicar of Avenbury dies and witnesses have reported seeing the enactment of the death of these vicars while standing on the tower of St Andrew's.

R

Red Lion Square, Holborn, WC1

The ghosts of Oliver Cromwell, his son-in-law Henry Ireton and John Bradshaw (president of the court that sentenced Charles I) have been seen walking abreast from south to north, deep in conversation. Their bodies were taken out of Westminster Abbey after the Restoration and hanged at Tyburn. After the disinterment, their corpses were first taken to Red Lion Square (then Field) as there were gallows there. It is believed that their bodies were desecrated before being taken to Tyburn, hence the haunting.

Red Lion Street, WC1: The Dolphin

The pub was bombed during an air raid in 1915 by a Zeppelin dirigible, killing three people and injuring several others. The building was completely devastated

Red Lion Square, where Oliver Cromwell, Henry Ireton and John Bradshaw walk and talk.

but the clock was salvaged and now hangs in the bar of the new building. The hands of the clock remain stopped at the time the bombing took place: 10.40pm. After the pub has closed, the landlord and staff have heard strange, low noises coming from the clock in the form of a chilling, subdued whistle. The whistling continues for some time, getting gradually lower and lower in tone until it finally ceases.

Regent Street, W1: Argyle Rooms

During the 19th century these rooms were regularly frequented by the gentry. One young lady arrived there one night to attend a concert, but had to be taken straight home because she was feeling unwell. She refused for a long time to discuss what it was that had upset her on that particular evening, but she finally confessed that she had seen the dead body of someone she knew lying on the floor, covered by a cloth mantle. Her family and friends had difficulty in believing what she was telling them, assuming that she was making a fuss about nothing. However, when they received notice in writing that the man in question had been drowned in Southampton, they gave her sighting more credence.

Richmond, Surrey: The Richmond Theatre

Three ghosts haunt this Victorian theatre. Most notable among them is the apparition of a director who fell from the balcony of the dress circle in 1939.

The second ghost seems to have a strange habit of walking into the women's lavatories. When challenged or investigated it simply disappears.

The third is the ghost of a woman who appears fleetingly behind the stage and then disappears. The chief electrician said:

> …for no reason all the hairs on the back of your neck will stand up. There are certain parts of the theatre that feel very different. You can go for a walk along one of the corridors and the atmosphere can just change. Over the years different people have come forward with the same story. New ushers, who have never worked in the theatre, have said what they have seen and felt. It is the same story that keeps recurring time and time again, so there must be something in it.

In the late 1980s a clairvoyant spent a night in the theatre and confirmed that it is, indeed, haunted by three different spirits.

St George's Drive, SW1: The Georgian House Hotel

William Chinnery Mitchell erected the building that houses the Georgian House Hotel in 1851 as his private dwelling. Mitchell designed the whole of the area of Pimlico, which was quite a feat as at the time it was boggy marshland. The top floor of the hotel is haunted by the ghosts of children who have actually conversed with

one of the managers of the hotel. She assured them that they were quite welcome but that she would prefer that they did not venture into the lower floors as children there would be frightened of them. Several other ghosts have been seen here, including a male ghost that has been seen in one of the basement staff rooms. A guest in one of the top rooms awoke with the feeling that he was being watched by another male apparition, and a third manifestation of a man has been seen standing in the kitchen. The direct descendants of Mitchell still run the hotel today.

St James's Palace, Pall Mall, SW1

The Duchess of Mazarin and Madame de Beauclair were the mistresses of Charles II and James II, and were given a suite of apartments here for their retirement. Both had an abiding interest in the afterlife. Mazarin died first, having accurately predicted her death to the minute, and within hours of dying made contact with the surviving de Beauclair. Mazarin appeared to her friend as if she were swimming rather than walking round the bed and told her that she would die between 12am and 1am that night, which she did.

In 1810, Ernest Augustus, Duke of Cumberland, fifth son of George III, was said to have murdered a servant called Sellis. Ernest had seduced Sellis's daughter and made her pregnant. In a rage and to cover up the scandal, he slit Sellis's throat and

St James's Palace was the retirement home of the the Duchess of Mazarin and Madame de Beauclair.

injured himself to make it appear that Sellis had tried to assassinate him and then commit suicide. Sellis's ghost can still be seen walking around the palace, his throat cut from ear to ear, accompanied by the smell of fresh blood.

St James's Palace is also haunted by the smell of fresh blood.

St James's Park, SW1: Birdcage Walk

The headless figure of a woman, dressed in a red and white striped gown, has been seen walking from the Cockpit Steps down to the canal. For some years, only officers and men of the Coldstream Guards saw this apparition, although today she seems to be happy for anyone to see her. She is thought to be the ghost of the wife of a sergeant in the Coldstreamers, who was murdered by her husband. He threw her body into a canal that ran through the park and buried her head nearby.

Queen Anne, whose statue stands close to Queen Anne's Gate, is said to

Birdcage Walk, St James's Park, where Queen Anne visits her statue each year.

dismount from the statue at midnight on the anniversary of her death (1 August) each year. She then proceeds to do three circuits of the street before climbing back onto the statue.

A headless woman haunts the lake in the park. Witnesses have seen the terrifying figure surface from the lake and walk across the water to the dry land, where she starts to run in a frantic manner before disappearing near some bushes. Theory has it that this apparition is searching for the head that was cut off by her husband and buried before he flung the remainder of her dead body into the lake.

Birdcage Walk, St James's Park, where a headless female apparition rises from the lake.

St James's Park, SW1: Lancaster House

This is the site of the former London Museum. The treasures of an unknown murdered woman may well have triggered off a series of haunting episodes revolving around the former base of the London Museum at Lancaster House and at the home of one of the curators. Excavations at a warehouse site near St Paul's Cathedral unearthed a wooden box containing over 150 items of jewellery, including rings, necklaces and pendants. These were taken to the London Museum and were initially kept at the house of one of the curators. The jewels were delivered on a warm, June evening at about 6pm. By 10pm the curator and his family found the room in which the jewels had been deposited to be very cold. An expert in the

Jewellery that caused ghostly activity was housed in the London Museum in St James's Park.

paranormal was called in the following day and, after having looked at the jewels, he told the family that a tall, thin man, wearing Elizabethan-style clothing, was present. The expert said that the apparition seemed to be angry because the jewels had been disturbed. Some years later, after the jewels had been rehoused in the London Museum, another paranormal expert described the same angry apparition, who this time stood behind the curator's daughter. The daughter's only connection to the jewels was that she had helped her father to clean them shortly after they had been delivered. A third paranormal expert stated that she could see a psychic residue of blood on the jewels and believed that the man seen by the other two experts had murdered the woman who owned them.

Cockpit Steps, St James's Park, has the ghost of a headless female.

St James's Place, SW1: No.19

Ann Pearson died in 1858, followed by her sister Harriet in 1864. Harriet had become very ill in November 1864, and was nursed by her servant Eliza Quintin. Harriet's nieces, Mrs Coppinger and Miss Emma Pearson, were also on hand to

No.19 St James's Place, where Ann Pearson came to collect her sister Harriet.

help. During the night of 23 December, they all saw a woman going into Harriet's room wearing a shawl and a black cap. They rushed into the room to see who it was, only to find Harriet alone. She told them, just before she died the following evening, that it had been her sister coming to take her away.

St James's Street, SW1

During the 19th century one of the houses in this street had a reputation for being haunted and having evil connections, so much so that it remained empty for a number of years. Not knowing about the reputation of the house, a young man returned from abroad and spent the night in the upper rooms. He only managed to stay there one night, so disturbed was he by the fact that he was watched the whole time by eyes peering through the curtains of the bed.

Some time later the house was being refurbished by a group of workmen. The supervisor decided to inspect the property while the workers were away and went into the house alone. He began to climb the stairs when he heard a footstep behind him. When he looked around there was nobody to be seen. Feeling frightened, the man proceeded to make a lot of noise in the drawing room of the house by banging a chair down on the floor. To the man's horror, the unseen apparition mirrored the exact noises and, quite naturally, he fled from the house.

St Martin's Lane, WC2: Coliseum Theatre

The Coliseum is the largest theatre in London and Frank Matcham designed it in 1904. The manifestation of a World War One British officer has been seen walking down the dress circle area and heading for the second row, just as performances are about to start. It is said that he was killed in action on 3 October 1918. The night before he returned to the front, he had spent the evening at the theatre.

A lady dressed in black has also been seen in and around the area of the theatre. It is believed that she was once a housekeeper in one of the houses in the area and used to frequent the theatre.

The distinctive voice of Sir John Barbirolli, one of the most important conductors of the last century, has also been heard at this theatre in its phantom form.

St Martin's Lane, WC2: Duke of York's Theatre

In 1949, the actress Thora Hird was using a short-backed bolero jacket as part of her costume. To begin with it fitted well, but the more she wore it the tighter it became. Erica Foyle, her understudy, felt the same tightness around the chest and arms. She even saw the apparition of a young woman in the mirror, wearing the same jacket. Others tried it on too; the wife of the play's director was left with red weals on the side of her throat. A medium was able to relate the story of the jacket

Duke of York's Theatre, St Martin's Lane, where the short bolero jacket perplexed actresses.

to them: the had jacket belonged to a Victorian girl called Edith Merryweather, who was murdered by a man who had held her head in a water butt until she drowned.

The theatre also boasts the ghost of Violet Melnotte-Wyatt, who was married to the theatre's first manager, Frank Wyatt. Violet was an actress, the first proprietor of the theatre in 1892 and the owner of the Amber Ale Brewery. At that time the theatre was known as the Trafalgar Square Theatre. She has been seen to mingle with members of the audience, particularly on the first night of a new performance.

St Michael's Alley, EC3: The George and Vulture

The upper rooms of this pub and eating house are haunted by an unknown Victorian lady. She has been seen silently floating around the rooms and corridors of the upper floor, wearing a long, grey dress.

St Paul's Cathedral, EC1

The Kitchener Memorial Chapel, formerly the All Souls' Chapel, commemorates those lost during World War One. The apparition of a former clergyman, whistling in a high-pitched tone, appears for a few seconds and then disappears into the wall. The ghost is said to have grey hair and the point of his disappearance was solved when a hidden doorway was found, leading to a staircase and the dome. When the chapel was re-dedicated after World War One the door that concealed a winding wooden staircase was found which led to a secret room. It had probably remained

St Paul's Cathedral has a grey-haired ghost that disappears through a secret doorway.

sealed and undiscovered for centuries. Despite this discovery, witnesses still report feeling a cold chill in the area prior to seeing the clergyman heading toward them, his whistle getting louder and louder, before he disappears through the doorway. The Deanery of St Paul's is also haunted by strange footsteps and other noises in the middle of the night.

St Thomas's Church, off Regent Street, W1

In 1921, Revd Clarence May, the assistant priest at the church, arrived to prepare to say Mass. He saw another priest, wearing a black cassock, at prayer in front of the altar. He went over to greet the priest, but he vanished, and the door to the sacristy was locked. When May unlocked the door, the sacristy was empty. Three other witnesses saw the same apparition, and it was later discovered that the manifestation was that of a 19th-century priest.

Sadlers Wells Theatre, EC1

Joe Grimaldi, the stage clown, died in 1837. It was this theatre that helped establish his act and popularity. His ghost has been seen in one of the boxes in the theatre, sometimes sitting behind members of the audience. He is clearly identifiable by his white face paint.

Sanderstead, Surrey: Selsdon Park Hotel, Addington Road

Set in over 200 acres of land, this neo-Jacobean mansion has been much extended over the centuries. It is believed that there was a building here during the Anglo-Saxon period and it is mentioned in the Domesday Book. The Archbishop of Canterbury gave the house to the Knights Templar in the mid-1100s. The present building probably dates from around 1670 and was the work of Christopher Bowyer, who is buried in the churchyard of Sanderstead Church. At the end of the 18th century the Smith family converted the building to the Gothic style. This work was completed in 1809. It then returned to its religious connections, becoming the home of Bishop Thorold. At some point part of the old Dominican Blackfriars' monastery was removed to the site and rebuilt as Blackfriars' Arch. The haunting occurs in the Tudor corridor, said to be the oldest part of the hotel, but has also been seen in two of the bars. It is believed that the ghost is that of a servant who worked in the house and committed suicide in the 1930s. She is referred to as the grey lady. What is perplexing about the story is that other witnesses have described the ghost as wearing Elizabethan or Tudor dress rather than clothing that could be associated with a 1930s servant. Two members of staff saw a small woman from behind after hearing the doors at one end of the corridor open on their own. When they ran to investigate she had gone, but they both described the atmosphere as being cold and clammy. On another occasion the same grey lady was seen to walk through the bed in room 235. What is particularly significant about the eyewitness reports is that the manifestation seems to be unaware of the fact that the modern flooring is higher as a result of central heating installation. Therefore the witnesses have described her as only appearing from the ankles up.

Shepherd's Bush, W12: The Bush Theatre

The ghost of Dylan Thomas, the Welsh-born writer and poet, has been seen standing at the back of the auditorium with a drink in his hand. There was once a BBC rehearsal room on the top floor of the Shepherd's Bush Hotel which was much used by Dylan Thomas when he worked for the BBC, before he died in New York in 1953.

Shooters Hill, SE18

In January 1844, a labourer unearthed a skeleton with a skull fracture. The body had not been buried long. It was surmised that there was a connection with the manifestation of a white lady that had been seen in the area. The Old Bull Hotel stood near here and when it was demolished they found an old pistol. The theory is that the woman was clubbed to death with the pistol and left to die. Witnesses passing this spot continue to hear a woman's cries for help.

Smithfield, EC1: No.33, Cock Lane

The ghost at this house is known as 'Scratching Fanny'. In 1759 Richard Parsons, his wife and their two daughters occupied the house. They let part of the house to William Kent, whose wife, Elizabeth, had died two years before, and he shared the accommodation with his sister-in-law, Frances, known as Fanny. The pair lived as man and wife. Following a row, Kent and Fanny moved to Clerkenwell, where Fanny died of smallpox in 1760. Noises then began waking the Parsons in the night. Mary Frazer, a servant, suggested that the knockings and tappings were a simple code and that it was Fanny and that she had been poisoned by William Kent. The latter took the Parsons to court in protest against the allegations that they made, and won. He was awarded a large sum of money and the Parsons were imprisoned. For several years the whole business of the death of Fanny was forgotten, particularly as Elizabeth Parsons, Richard's daughter, confessed to having caused the noises in the first place. However, in 1845 Fanny's coffin was opened and the corpse showed all the signs of death by arsenic poisoning and not smallpox. There is still some dispute about whether the ghost is actually that of Fanny or her sister Elizabeth, who objected to the fact that her husband was living with her sister.

In 1762 a pamphlet, written anonymously, but in fact by Oliver Goldsmith (1730–1774), entitled *The Mystery Revealed; Containing a Series of Transactions and*

Authentic Testimonials, Respecting the Supposed Cock Lane Ghost was published. It was as a result of a séance that he attended in one of the bedrooms of 33 Cock Lane that he wrote:

> To have a proper idea of this scene, as it is now carried on, the reader is to conceive a very small room with a bed in the middle, the girl, at the usual hour of going to bed, is undressed and put in with proper solemnity; the spectators are next introduced who sit looking at each other, suppressing laughter, and wait in silent expectation for their opening of the scene. As the ghost is a good deal offended at incredulity, the persons present are to conceal theirs, if they have any, as by this concealment they can only hope to gratify their curiosity. For if they show either before, or when the knocking is begun, a too prying, inquisitive, or ludicrous turn of thinking, the ghost continued usually silent, or, to use the expression of the house, Miss Fanny is angry. The spectators therefore have nothing for it, but to sit quiet and credulous, otherwise they must hear no ghost, which is no small disappointment to persons, who have come for no other purpose. The girl who knows, by some secret, when the ghost is to appear, sometimes apprises the assistants of its intended visitation. It first begins to scratch and then to answer questions, giving two knocks for a negative, and one for an affirmative. By this means it tells whether a watch, when held up, be white, blue, yellow, or black; how many clergymen are in the room, though in this sometimes mistaken; it evidently distinguishes white men from Negroes, with several other marks of sagacity; however, it is sometimes mistaken in questions of a private nature, when it deigns to answer them; for instance, the ghost was ignorant where she dined upon Mr Kent's marriage; how many of her relations were at the church upon the same occasion; but particularly she called her father John instead of Thomas, a mistake indeed a little extraordinary in a ghost; but perhaps she was willing to verify the old proverb, that it is a wise child that knows its own father.

Harry Price, writing in 1945 in his book *Poltergeist Over England* summed up his thoughts on the Cock Lane ghost:

> So I am inclined to think that perhaps, after all, there were some genuine phenomena in the Cock Lane affair. There was the usual young girl, so much in evidence in genuine poltergeist cases, and it seems incredible that so many people of culture and intelligence could have visited Elizabeth's bedroom night after night without once detecting imposture – as indeed they did on one occasion when the trick was so apparent. At dark séances fraud can remain undetected

for long periods. But not when a girl is in bed with people crowding round her and under a good light. It would be interesting to know what became of the Parsons family, especially the medium, Elizabeth. There is no record of any further 'trouble' either in Cock Lane or elsewhere.

Smithfield, EC1: St Bartholomew's Church

Rahere was King Henry I's court jester and in 1110, *en route* to Rome on a pilgrimage, he contracted malaria just three miles from the city. He vowed, standing on the same ground that St Peter was murdered on, that if he recovered from the malaria, the moment he returned to England he would found a church and hospital for the poor. While convalescing St Bartholomew appeared to him in a vision and told him that a hospital should be built at Smithfield. This was a strange choice as Smithfield at the time was a swamp. Rahere returned to England and, after securing the king's blessing, he started building works in 1123.

Rahere became the first prior of St Bartholomew's and died there in 1142, having seen the hospital grow and flourish in the 19 years since its establishment. Rahere's ghost has been seen on many occasions and at other times witnesses have simply heard his footsteps. The area of the haunting seems to be restricted to the church and one witness, a church helper, was continually perturbed by the fact that her elaborate flower arrangements always seemed to droop no matter what she did. When she explained her predicament to the rector, he told her that he had seen Rahere standing behind her on several occasions. Rahere, apparently, was something of a misogynist, and his ghost also seems to dislike women. One of the rectors also saw Rahere as a cowled figure standing in the church. When approached the ghost simply turned and walked toward the Lady Chapel. The rector followed him but the figure disappeared. From the various reports, from rectors, their wives, parishioners and visitors, Rahere is most likely to be seen near the altar. An additional and rather unusual story revolves around Rahere's tomb, which for many years was believed to be a place of healing for the faithful who prayed beside it. When his tomb was opened in 1865 one of the church workers became very ill. So strong was her belief in Rahere's healing abilities that she, apparently, stole into the church, removed Rahere's sandals and placed them near her bed while she slept. Within a short period of time her illness was cured and the sandals were returned.

In addition to the ghost of Rahere, a rector accompanying visitors to the church during the early 20th century saw the manifestation of a Reformation period priest. The ghost was delivering a sermon from the pulpit. The priest was very animated and his lips were moving as if speaking, but no sound was coming from him. The rector was the only one of the group to witness the apparition.

The gatehouse of the church also has a series of hauntings that are thought to reflect the executions and burnings that took place there at a place called The Elms. Several witnesses, while walking past this area at night, have described hearing ghostly cries, the sound of crackling faggots and the smell of charred flesh.

Smithfield, EC1: St Bartholomew's Hospital

The grey lady that has been seen in the area of Grace Ward is believed to be the apparition of a former nurse at the hospital. The nurse was responsible for caring for the patients in the psychiatric ward. Unfortunately she was killed by one of the patients and, presumably, chooses to continue her work even in death.

Separated by a road from the hospital, Charterhouse, the original house of the famous school, was founded in 1611 by Sir Thomas Sutton as a hospital for poor boys, fulfilling his lifelong wish to found a benevolent institution. The headless ghost of Thomas Howard, 4th Duke of Norfolk, has been seen in the building. He owned it before Thomas Sutton. After Howard's wife, Lady Dacre, died, the duke became involved in a plot to marry Mary Queen of Scots and he was executed in 1572. His apparition is said to walk down the staircase of the Great Hall. The courtyards are also said to be haunted by the apparition of an unknown monk who wanders or drifts over the cobbled yard.

Apparently the hospital was the scene of the murder of a nurse in years gone by. She was murdered in the lift and it is believed that it is her manifestation that causes the lift to malfunction at times. Now known as 'the Coffin Lift', it appears, at times, to have a will of its own and regularly takes the occupants to the basement of the hospital, regardless of which button they have pressed. A phantom lift has also been reported as following witnesses up the stairs that run to the side of the 'actual' lift.

Smithfield Market, EC1

During the 17th century a lawyer named Mallet died from food poisoning after eating meat from the Smithfield market or from Whitechapel or Eastcheap. His ghost has been seen, dressed in his lawyer's gown and pointed shoes, on Saturday evenings. When his manifestation first appeared at the market it is said to have tormented the butchers, some of whom attempted to frighten away the spectre with their knives. It would appear that Mallet was unsure that his death had been a result of the meat from Smithfield, for his apparition also appeared to the butchers of Whitechapel and Eastcheap.

Smithfield Market, EC1: Ye Old Red Cow, Long Lane

Situated very close to Smithfield Market, this pub, has, for many years, served the market porters and been open from the early hours of the morning in order to meet their needs. A former landlord, Irishman Dick O'Shea, is said to haunt the pub by presenting himself in the same manner that he did every day of his life. Apparently the pub used to have a balcony and Dick would sit in his rocking chair and watch his customers from above.

Southwark, SE1: Bishop's House

The ghost of a very sad-looking old Polish woman was seen at this house, where she was reported to have died. Apparently the staff who worked here found her manifestation extremely depressing, so much so that they forced the bishop to perform an exorcism that, apparently, put the poor woman's soul to rest.

Southwark, SE1: Deadman's Place

According to the *Full and True Relation of the Appearing of a Dreadful Ghost*, published by the borough of Southwark in 1690, a pub used to stand in one of the buildings in the former Deadman's Place. The landlord and his wife, together with their children, lived a hard life without much money for several years. Apparently the landlord's wife was prone to outbursts of temper and had several arguments with him and their neighbours. She died quite early in life and unexpectedly but, according to the *Full and True Relation*, the landlord looked forward to a more peaceful existence. However, it would appear that his wife, despite her death, had different ideas. She began to haunt her husband. One night she appeared to her husband, accompanied by loud and frightening noises, and she hit him on the arm with a saucepan, hurting him so badly that he could not use the arm for several days.

This type of ghostly experience continued for several nights and ultimately the man moved out of the pub to the house of friends nearby. This did not deter the wife, however, as she simply moved with him and brought with her several other ghostly friends. He moved again, this time even further away, but the determined ghost of his former wife followed him again. This time she grabbed him while he was in bed and he was reported to comment that her hand was perfectly formed. The end of this story is not known, but it is reported that the landlord consulted ministers to gain some spiritual consolation and save himself from insanity.

Southwark, SE1: London Bridge

The position occupied by London Bridge is a little way down-river from where the Old London Bridge was constructed, which served London between 1215 and 1832. In 1290 Edward I instituted a pogrom against the Jewish community in England and demanded that they be expelled from the country. One group of refugees hired a boat to escape imprisonment and death. It was due to set sail from just below the Old London Bridge. Unfortunately the boat was beached on the bank. The passengers disembarked and stood on the riverbank waiting for the tide to release the ship. As the water rose the captain made it back on to the boat, but the passengers were left stranded on the riverbank and were drowned. Not only does this part of the river have a strange eeriness about it, but other witnesses also claim to have heard the screams of the drowning people.

Southwark, SE1: The Anchor Inn, Bank End

Although this 18th-century public house was extensively refurbished in the 1980s, it still retains much of the atmosphere of its less-than-salubrious clientele of the past. Not all the customers were unpleasant, as the pub was also said to be a favourite watering hole of Samuel Johnson. The haunting seems to date back to the time when the crews of the barges and other ships moored along the Thames would use the pub as one of their favoured drinking dens. This was the period of the press gang and many of Her Majesty's finest sailors were once unwilling and often unwitting 'volunteers'. Poor recruitment, disease, death and desertion, meant that the navy was often short of men. Press gangs were armed naval men who would enter a pub looking for likely lads who were prepared to join the crew. In many cases they found not only a negative response from the customers but a positively hostile one too. Nevertheless, they would often resort to kidnapping new recruits or cudgelling them into unconsciousness so that the poor victim would find himself several miles out to sea before they came to. On this one occasion the press gangs homed in on a particular customer who owned a dog. In the ensuing melée, the dog attacked the press gang and one of the sailors slammed the door to prevent the dog from biting him and severed its tail in the process. The dog bounded off into the distance, never to be seen again. It is said that the ghost of this unfortunate canine can be seen wandering around the pub, perhaps looking for the lost part of its anatomy.

Other witnesses have heard a dog scratching against a door and others claim to have heard to the sound of a dog's padding feet.

Southwark, SE1: The George, Borough High Street

This public house that was built in 1677 is a magnificent galleried coaching inn. It is haunted by the ghost of Miss Murray, who was the landlady from the end of the 19th century until the beginning of the 20th century. She managed the inn at a very awkward time for coaching premises. The railways were beginning to be developed across the country and it seemed that it would only be a matter of time before the purpose of her establishment became redundant. Many of the other coaching inns in the area were demolished and it was only after three galleries at the George were similarly dismantled that her ghost began to make an appearance. It seems that she has a particular problem with technological innovations. Electrical equipment constantly fails, computers and tills seem to cease functioning for no apparent reason and whenever electricians or maintenance engineers are called in they can find no fault with any of the equipment. Members of staff claim to have actually seen the rather indistinct form of Miss Murray floating around their rooms as if shrouded in a mist in the early hours of the morning. She does not appear to direct any particular malice toward humans.

Southwark, SE1: The Market Porter, Park Street

Regulars and neighbours of this Victorian public house have seen strange, floating figures moving in and around the building after closing time. While it may be suspected that either the witnesses or the shapes in question have had a little too much to drink, it is the experiences of one of the landlords that, perhaps, put the hauntings into perspective. Having cashed up one evening the landlord went to the upper bar to find that the till was running by itself. This was despite the fact that there was no other person in the room. On another occasion, having completed the cleaning up chores for the night, the landlord switched off and then unplugged the glass-washing machine. When he went downstairs the following morning he found the door open and water gushing onto the floor.

The landlord attributes his experiences to the presence of a rather unusual ethnic artefact – an African goat's head – which adorns the top of the door frame in the back bar. Several people have told him that the unpleasant item attracts evil spirits.

Southwark, SE1: The Operating Theatre Museum, St Thomas's Street

In 1861 Florence Nightingale established her School of Nursing here at the site of St Thomas's Hospital. The operating theatre, at the top of a winding, wooden staircase, in the roof of a church, was first opened in 1821. The museum replicates exactly what a surgery would have looked like in the 19th century and among its myriad of exhibits is a photograph that purports to show, quite clearly, the ghost of Florence Nightingale standing in the background. The staff that work at the museum have heard footsteps coming up the stairs after the museum has closed and on other occasions have heard running steps. Although none of the present staff can claim to have seen Florence Nightingale, the inexplicable sounds have occurred on numerous occasions and there seems to be no credible reason for them.

Stanmore, Middlesex: Old Church Farm

This was a former rectory and the ghost of a parson haunts it. He has been seen to rise from his grave opposite the farm, walk toward the farm, enter the house and then make the return trip. Witnesses report hearing knocking and other noises and the ghost seems particularly interested if there is an ill person in the house. In nearby Honeypot Lane, witnesses have spoken of a rushing sound and the feeling that something has brushed past them. It could be that this is related to a battle that took place here between the Romans and the Britons shortly after Caesar's invasion.

Stepney, E8: Cephas Street

The Bass sales office now occupies the building but it was formerly a doctor's surgery. In 1980 the staff complained that the offices felt unpleasantly cold, making the hairs on their arms stand on end, and that they could smell a 'sweet, sickly smell'. After some research it was discovered that a pregnant woman had been involved in a road accident outside the surgery, and despite medical attention she had died, although the baby was saved. The cause of this cold, smelly presence was attributed to the accident.

Stepney, E8: Hanbury Street

Annie Chapman was mutilated and murdered by the 19th-century serial killer Jack the Ripper, and appears here in phantom form. Annie was the second of Jack's victims. She was found dead on 8 September 1888 in Hanbury Street. It is interesting to note that she has been positively identified. Extensive news coverage made her face very familiar to the public for several years.

Stepney, E8: London Jewish Hospital

In 1977 a hazy figure used to brush past the nurses while they were on duty at the hospital and walk in and out of their rest room at night. A rabbi was called in to say prayers and it is believed that the ghost, a former patient, has now found rest.

Stepney, E1: Magistrates Court, Aylward Street

The ghost of Lillian Browne, a former matron at Thames Magistrates Court, haunts this building. She has been seen on a number of occasions, particularly in and around the area of the Matron's Room. Lillian was matron for 26 years and did not take retirement until the age of 77. Her work must have been her main reason for staying alive, because she died only seven weeks after retiring.

Stepney, E8: Regents Canal Dock, Ratcliff Wharf

The 19th-century vicar of Ratcliff Cross opened a lodging house for seamen. It is now widely believed that he was a serial murderer, who killed his lodgers in their sleep for their money. The apparition of a grey or white-haired vicar has been seen on a regular basis for around a hundred years. He wears clerical clothes, with gaiters that button at the sides, and he carries a walking stick.

Strand, WC2: Coutts Bank

This was the site where Elizabeth I had the 4th Duke of Norfolk beheaded for treason because of his involvement in the plot to marry Mary, Queen of Scots, on 2 June 1572. An exorcism was carried out in 1993 in order to calm the restless spirit that has appeared headless and moaning on numerous occasions. The medium Eddie Burks made contact with the ghost and found out that it was, in fact, that of Thomas Howard, the Duke of Norfolk, who asked for help in putting his spirit to rest. Prayers were offered at a large gathering and no further activity has been reported since then.

One of the ancestors of the Coutts family has also been seen in the vicinity of the bank. Baroness Burdett-Coutts has been witnessed walking along the Strand dressed in her Edwardian dress.

Strand, WC2: Law Courts

According to stories that surround this building, the site is built on what used to be a 'rabbit warren' type maze of passageways and alleys. Some of the local children used to earn a living by escorting strangers to the area through this maze. Apparently one visitor refused to pay for the privilege of being escorted and set off to his chosen destination on his own, but unfortunately he was never seen again. It is the ghost of this lost soul that has been witnessed around the current building, formally called the Royal Courts of Justice.

Strand, WC2: Rules Restaurant, Maiden Lane

Named by its founder, Thomas Rule, in the late 18th century, this restaurant has been the favourite eating-place of famous and aristocratic people for hundreds of years. In fact, it is said that a special doorway was built in the premises so that Edward II and Lillie Langtry could arrive and leave the restaurant in secret. However, it is possibly not the ghost of an aristocrat that haunts the building, or more specifically, the ladies' toilet. Apparently one of the cubicle doors is often heard to be slammed shut and the toilet is flushed despite the fact that the toilet is unoccupied. There is no known explanation for this strange haunting.

Strand, WC2: Savoy Hill House, Savoy Hill

The actress Billie Carlton died in a flat here shortly after celebrating at the Victory Ball in November 1918. Subsequently the BBC used the building as their headquarters.

The structure, part of which was formerly the home of the actress, was converted into offices. Numerous witnesses over a period of years have seen doors in the area of the actress's former home open and close while others have reported feeling a strange presence in that part of the building.

Coutts Bank, the Strand, where the beheaded Duke of Norfolk's manifestation was exorcised.

Somerset House is haunted by Horatio Nelson.

Strand, WC2: Somerset House

This building was formerly the Admiralty and is haunted by none other than Horatio Nelson. His ghost appears, clearly identifiable in full uniform, but what is interesting about the apparition is that the ghost does not have an arm and Nelson appears to look frail. This is unlike some of his more hearty hauntings elsewhere. There is also a strange cloud manifestation above his apparition's head as he crosses the quadrangle and disappears if approached. Nelson is also said to haunt the Gun Inn in Docklands.

Strand, WC2: The Adelphi Theatre

William Terris, whose ghost also appears at Covent Garden underground station, was actually murdered here by a bit-part actor who was jealous of his success. Richard Prince murdered him on 16 December 1897 while Terris was appearing in *Secret Service*. Terris died in the arms of his mistress, Jessie Milward. It is reported that his dying words were 'I'll be back'. His apparition appears bathed in green light and clad in a grey suit with an old-fashioned collar and white gloves. Electricians have seen him walking through a whole row of seats and disappearing through a wall. His former dressing room is said to reverberate with rapping noises but this may not necessarily be William. It is remembered, however, that Terris used to tap

on the door of his leading lady's dressing room to let her know that he was going elsewhere. In 1928 an actress reported a strange phenomenon that had occurred in her dressing room, which she later found out to be the one that Jessie Milward had used. Apparently she was lying on a chaise longue when she saw a green light appear and suddenly felt she was being rocked from side to side on the piece of furniture. This phenomenon was coupled with two loud knocking noises.

Strand, WC2: The George Tavern

The ghost here is named after the building itself and George is a frequent visitor, particularly in the area of the cellar. He takes the form of a harmless cavalier, who merely stands and watches those carrying out their duties on the beer barrels that are stored in the cellar of the building.

Strand, WC2: The Lyceum Theatre, Aldwych

A most macabre apparition appears from time to time in one of the former stalls seats. The haunting seems to relate to a man whose family owned the land on which the original theatre was built in 1772. This land was owned by the 1st Duke of Exeter, who was executed in 1400 for conspiring against Henry IV, but it is believed that the haunting is of a later member of the family, namely Henry Courtenay,

executed in 1538, or that of a family member beheaded at the behest of Cromwell. On certain occasions, looking down from one of the boxes, you may see a woman calmly sitting in one of the seats with a severed head on her lap. On other occasions the woman discreetly pulls a shawl over her lap to hide the hideous manifestation.

The Lyceum Theatre, where a ghostly woman sits with a severed head in her lap.

Strand, WC2: The Nell Gwynne, Bull Inn Court

The ghost of an old man, who evidently wants to keep things exactly as they have been for years, is believed to be a former landlord of this pub. A medium was called into the building after several witnesses had claimed to feel coldness in the air at certain times and in certain areas of the bar. Other witnesses, particularly male customers, had felt someone tap the back pocket of their trousers, but when turning to investigate the customers could see nobody. Since the medium visited the pub it has changed hands several times and often those landlords who have tried to make changes have left unexpectedly without reason.

Strand, WC2: The Wig and Pen Club

Situated opposite the Law Courts on the Strand, this building was once a solicitor's office during the Victorian period. The haunting apparently relates to a 19th-century solicitor's clerk, or a solicitor, who died in unexplained circumstances on the premises. His ghost can be heard walking around the ground floor at 2am most mornings. The actual building is one of the few Tudor period houses that survived the Great Fire of London. It is believed that the foundations retain remains of a Roman dwelling, attesting to its long history.

This half-timbered building is said to be haunted by the ghost of Oliver Cromwell. When Charles II came to the throne in 1660 he had the former Lord Protector, and executor of his father, disinterred and his head stuck on a spike by Temple Bar. Cromwell's ghost is said to return occasionally, presumably in search of his head, despite the fact that his head is reported to be buried in the chapel of Sidney Sussex College, Cambridge.

Temple, EC4

Temple was originally built by the Knights Templar, who were the earliest founders of the military orders, and remained there from 1184 until their order was disbanded in 1312. It was then leased to Aymerde de Valence, Earl of Pembroke. In 1608, King James I gave the property to the Inner and Middle Temples. The ghost that haunts the Temple is Sir Henry Hawkins, a barrister who later became Lord Brampton, 'The Hanging Judge'. He is seen dressed in wig and gown, gliding through the cloisters with papers under his arm. Some years ago, a perfectly

Fountains Court, Temple. Lord Brampton haunts the surrounding buildings.

preserved skeleton was found in a wall near the roof, which is believed to be over 200 years old.

Temple, EC4: Ye Olde Cock Tavern, nr Fleet Street

A portrait of Oliver Goldsmith, the Irish-born writer and playwright, hangs on one of the walls of the first floor of this building and this helped a witness to identify the ghostly apparition she had seen. Goldsmith's ghostly head, hovering at her face level and grinning, appeared to one of the barmaids during the 1980s at the back door of the pub. Goldsmith is buried in the churchyard of the church of Saint Mary nearby, and a memorial to him was erected in Westminster Abbey.

Thamesmead, SE28: Tavey Bridge

During the Battle of Britain, a Spitfire pilot was shot down and crashed on Erith Marshes. The manifestation of the pilot, dressed in his RAF uniform, walks around the Tavey Bridge area. He is described as being tall and dark. The apparition is known to make banging noises in the local butcher's shop and has even made an appearance in a neighbour's bedroom.

Tottenham, N15: Bruce Castle

This is the former home of Rowland Hill, founder of the Post Office and the Penny

Post. The building dates back to Elizabethan times, and is on the site of an older house constructed by the father of Robert Bruce. In the 17th century, Lord Coleraine imprisoned his beautiful wife Constantia in a chamber above the entrance. At her wits end, she took her child in her arms and jumped from the balustrade on 3 November 1680. Constantia's screams can be heard on the anniversary of her death.

Strange ghostly figures in 18th-century costume have also been seen in the grounds, disappearing into the wall of the building. This manifestation was witnessed by two independent pairs of people in July 1971, and on the second occasion, when the figures were approached they melted into the walls of the building.

Tower Hill, EC3

The aftermath of a full execution seems to be the manifestation that has appeared here on a number of occasions, particularly once during World War Two. A sentry, guarding the area at the time, watched a procession of men pass by. The figures were later identified as being mediaeval sheriff of London's guards and priests. They were carrying a stretcher with a corpse on it. The head looked as if it had been severed. Since then the manifestation has regularly appeared in this location.

Tower of London, EC3

Steeped in history, this magnificent structure teems with ghosts that mirror both the royal and ancestral heritage of the country. At Traitor's Gate Thomas Becket's ghost is said to have struck the structure twice, reducing it to rubble. The room dedicated to Becket's memory has poltergeist activity in the form of doors opening and closing of their own accord, the sound of a monk's sandals 'flapping' against the floor and the cries of an unknown baby.

A 'strange-looking figure' has been seen very close to the area where executions used to take place. The man, who was wearing drab clothes that the witness assumed were of World War Two utility type, walked with a bowed head and vanished after only a short time.

In the Bloody Tower the ghosts of King Edward V and his brother Richard, Duke of York, possibly murdered by Richard III, have been seen standing hand-in-hand, clad in nightgowns. Bones thought to be their skeletons were discovered in 1674 and given a proper burial.

A face has been seen looking from one of the windows of St Thomas's Tower by staff and visitors to the Tower.

In the Martin Tower Edmund Swifte saw a glass tube, which phased from white to blue, on a single occasion in 1817. George Boleyn, the brother of Anne, was hung, drawn and quartered here and his phantom presents itself in the upper rooms of the Tower. The unseen hands of Thomas Percy, who was imprisoned in the Martin Tower for his involvement in the Gunpowder Plot, push unsuspecting visitors down the steps. This Tower also boasts the ghost of a bear.

Northumberland Walk is the home of the ghost of the Earl of Northumberland, who exercised here prior to his execution.

Anne Boleyn haunts the Queen's House, where she was kept until her execution, having been seen by several different people, including sentries that have attempted to attack the apparition with bayonets. She appears here on the anniversary of her death, 19 May. She is also seen outside the chapel and Beefeaters have reported strange lights flickering in the middle of the night. One witness also reported seeing a procession of Tudor courtiers gliding along the aisle of the chapel led by a headless woman. They disappeared into a wall.

The shadow of an executioner's axe is said to pass over Tower Green and define itself on the White Tower. This is thought to be connected to the execution of Cardinal Pole's mother Margaret, the Countess of Salisbury, in 1541. The screams that have been heard in this area are thought to be the re-enactment of her execution, at which she fought with the executioner who chased her around the scaffold. Guards within the White Tower have also experienced ghostly happenings. One man experienced a feeling of being crushed, another had a black cloak flung over his head and twisted around his neck, and a third was spoken to by an unseen ghost.

Guildford Dudley's ghost has been seen both in the Beauchamp Tower and on Tower Hill. He was the fifth son of John Dudley and was married to Lady Jane Grey. He was tried at Guildhall on 13 November 1553 and found guilty of treason. It is reported that he wept on the way to the scaffold. Lady Jane Grey has also been seen in the Beauchamp Tower. She had watched her husband being executed and her apparition re-enacts her own fate, completed on the same day. She has been seen on the anniversary of her execution and is said to float on a cloud of shimmering mist, and glide along the battlements before disappearing.

Sir Walter Raleigh's ghost appears as a solid form that remains for only a short time before it disappears. He was imprisoned in the Tower from 1603 until 1618. Several yeomen have seen him peering into the guardroom. Both Cardinal Wolsey and Thomas Wentworth, Earl of Strafford, have also appeared in years gone by to those awaiting execution in the confines of the Tower.

The strange and frightening apparition of a giant brown bear has also been reported. In 1864 a soldier saw the bear and lunged at it with his bayonet. It is believed that the ghost of the bear relates to the bear-baiting shows that used to be arranged in the grounds of the Tower.

Ghostly choirs have been heard and numerous other poltergeist activities have been reported, including white smoke rising and changing shape out of one of the canons.

The Middle Tower is the home of the sound of pacing footsteps that have been heard to travel back and forth along the battlements.

The Byward Tower was the place of a sighting in the 1980s. A yeoman, while on duty during the night, saw two beefeaters dressed in clothes from a much earlier period than his own. They were standing in the tower, talking to one another animatedly, while enjoying a smoke of their pipes, one on either side of the fireplace.

Henry VI was imprisoned in the Wakefield Tower and murdered by unknown hands on 21 May 1471. His ghostly apparition can be seen on the anniversary of his death. He is said to pace pitifully around the room with a sad and pale expression on his face and when the clock completes its midnight chimes he disappears again into the walls.

The Salt Tower was the final resting place of Henry Walpole, who was imprisoned here in 1593, but it is not known if the strange yellow glow that fills the room is related to him. Visitors have also heard prayers said in a low, whispering voice and felt the ice-cold touch of fingers on their necks.

Twickenham, Middlesex: St Margaret's Churchyard

Alexander Pope, the poet and satirist (1688–1744) was buried here, but did not haunt the site until 1830 when someone stole his skull. Following this incident his

The Tower of London from across the Thames. The Tower is steeped in history and has multiple ghosts.

hunchbacked ghost has been seen walking around the churchyard and church. What is odd about it is that he talks to himself and coughs a lot. Even when he has not been seen, witnesses have reported hearing the slightly uneven sound of footsteps inside the church.

Vauxhall, SE1: The Morpeth Arms

The pub is on the site of the former Millbank Prison and it is believed that prisoners were once housed in what is now the cellar area of the pub. They waited there until they were transported to Australia. One of the prisoners, clearly unable to cope with the prospect of imprisonment and transportation, took his own life down there by hanging himself. The cellars have strange cold spots and smells that may also be related to the haunting. Although nothing has been seen, a strange presence is definitely at work in this place. One witness has reported seeing beer stains unaccountably appearing on the ceiling and having bottles snatched from his hands.

Villiers Street, WC2: Gordon's Wine Bar

It is not surprising that this particularly atmospheric pub has an unseen haunting. Some witnesses have reported the feeling of being watched and others claim to have been tapped on the shoulder by the invisible apparition while they have been in the bar.

Wandsworth, SW18: No.523, Wandsworth Road

This building is a former fish and chip restaurant, and while it was being used as such, a large black dog haunted it. The dog was thought to have belonged to a previous owner of the building and to have been killed in a road accident. The phantom dog would ignore the witnesses and walk through the shop and into the road, where it turned right and continued along to the main road, in the direction of the crossroads where the accident had occurred.

Wandsworth, SW18: Wandsworth Prison, Heathfield Street

Built in 1851, the prison is haunted by 'Wandsworth Annie', who was employed there as a cook and died in the 1870s. She is described as appearing to be middle-aged, with grey hair. She wears a Victorian grey dress, and staff and prisoners have seen her walking down the corridors.

Wanstead, E11

The terrifying apparitions of a man and woman have been seen in the churchyard.

The manifestation begins with a ghostly skeleton emerging, pushing a coffin cart. It approaches an ornate tomb in the middle of the cemetery, where a man in white joins it. The man walks over to the skeleton and puts his arms around it. The pair are husband and wife, and continue to embrace one another even in death.

Waterloo Road, SE1: The Old Vic

The Old Vic is haunted by two individuals; one is unknown but demonstrative, and the other is much more passive. The more active ghost is believed to be that of a well-loved actress from the past. She appears to be re-enacting one of her roles, that of Lady Macbeth, as she is seen wringing her bloody hands. An alternative suggestion is that she is the ghost of a murderess, who only appears to have theatrical connections by accident.

The other apparition is somewhat perplexing, as it is believed to be the ghost of William Shakespeare, who, apart from the fact that many of his plays have been performed here, would not have known of its existence in his time. None other than Sir Alec Guinness saw his apparition.

West Drayton, nr Uxbridge, Middlesex: West Drayton Church

Strange noises have been heard from the vaults under the church that holds the remains of the Pagets and the de Burghs. It is believed that two of the corpses either murdered one another or committed suicide together. Screams and knocking noises have been heard, and on one occasion a large black raven was seen sitting on one of the coffins. People with lanterns, sticks and stones scared it off. When it fell, exhausted, onto the ground, it vanished.

Westminster Abbey, SW1

Father Benedictus can be seen walking in the cloisters between 5 and 6pm. However, he does not actually walk, he glides, as the flagstones are somewhat lower than they were in his time. He is described as being a tall, lean and cowled figure. He was killed during the reign of Henry VIII at the Chapel of Pyx. The apparition made an appearance in front of visitors to the Abbey in 1900. Not only did they see him clearly, but they also talked to him for nearly half an hour. After they had finished the conversation with him he turned and floated back toward the cloisters where he disappeared through a wall. On another occasion in 1932 two lucky American tourists had another conversation with him. At the time they described him as being very kind and considerate and said that he had taken great pains to explain his own history and past.

The ghost of the Unknown Soldier has been seen near his tomb with its head bowed. He is dressed in the uniform of a World War One infantryman. Clearly the

identity of the Unknown Soldier is a mystery. An unidentified body was brought back from France on 11 November 1920 and given a full royal funeral in Westminster Abbey, in recognition of all those unaccounted-for servicemen that had died in the fighting. The coffin was buried in soil brought from Belgium, to signify the fact that many British soldiers had lost their lives defending Belgium's soil.

John Bradshaw, the judge who presided over the trial of Charles I, is also present in the abbey's triforium. He has surprised some tourists.

In the south cloisters, it is said that the seated statue of Daniel Pulteney, the politician, who is reading a book, has been seen to turn the pages.

Westminster Bridge, SW1

Although there is no explanation for the haunting that is said to take place at Westminster Bridge, witnesses claim to have seen a phantom boat approach and then go under the bridge. However, the phantom boat does not reappear on the other side of the bridge.

On New Year's Eve, at the stroke of midnight, a ghost thought to be the apparition of Jack the Ripper is said to leap from the bridge into the River Thames. Montague John Druitt was suspected of being the infamous murderer, and he is thought to have committed suicide by plunging into the Thames. His body was found on 31 December 1888. The true identity of Jack the Ripper has never been conclusively proved.

The west towers from the cloisters, Westminster Abbey.

Passage outside the Chapel of Pyx, Westminster Abbey, where Father Benedictus glides across the flagstones.

Westminster Cathedral, SW1

Although it is officially denied by the Catholic Church, this cathedral in Victoria is haunted by a black-robed figure that is said to disappear near the high altar. On one particular occasion when the cathedral was locked in July 1966, a sacristan on night duty saw it standing there and watched it fade into nothing.

Whitechapel, E1

The ghost of Jack the Ripper's first victim, Polly Nicholls, has been seen lying in the gutter near Whitechapel Station in Durward Street. Polly's body was discovered at 3.45am by the entrance to a stable yard on Bucks Row. She appeared as a dishevelled heap and her throat and abdomen had been slashed. Her ghostly apparition is described as lying huddled and surrounded by a strange aura.

Also in the Durward Street area 'a huddled figure, like that of a woman, emitting from all over it a ghostly light, frequently to be seen lying in the gutter' was reported by Elliott O'Donnell.

Whitehall, SW1: Admiralty House

In the late 18th century the Earl of Sandwich was the Lord Commissioner of the Admiralty and lived here with his mistress, Margaret Reay. Ms Reay was murdered by her previous lover, the Revd James Packman, on 7 April 1779, outside the Covent Garden Theatre where she had been attending a performance. Margaret's portrait hangs in the State Room, so it is not surprising that the many witnesses that have seen the apparition of a young woman in the main bedroom of what is now the Defence Secretary's flat, have positively identified her. During the late 1960s the then Defence Secretary, Denis Healey, lived in the flat. Newspaper reports claimed that Margaret was still present and that the Healey family had come to accept her as one of their own.

Whitehall, SW1: The Silver Cross

The manifestation of a little girl of the Tudor period appears in this public house. By all accounts the child is quite happy and playful and is often heard giggling and skipping around the building. During the late 1990s the then manager and members of his family also heard the voice of a woman apparition calling the name of a little boy on several occasions, although it is thought that this could have been the same apparition in play.

Whitehall Court, SW1: The National Liberal Club

Following much research and investigation in the 1890s, the cause of the strange noises heard at this building was blamed on one of the servants. Apparently the knocking noises that had been heard coming from within the walls of the building only ever occurred when the German-born servant was on the premises. The secretary of the club informed the girl that he had no alternative but to let her go and as soon as she vacated the premises for good the noises stopped.

Wilton Row, SW1: The Grenadier

In the early 19th century, a young Guards officer was caught cheating at cards in the pub. A fight broke out and he either fell or was pushed down the stairs. The fall killed him and his spirit returns in September each year on the anniversary of his death. The manifestation makes itself known as through poltergeist activity, by appearing as a strange shapeless blob, or as puffs of hot cigar smoke.

Wimbledon, SW19: Hillside

This is reputed to be the most haunted street in Wimbledon and there have been a number of different sightings here over the years. One explanation may be that the headquarters of a Spiritualist movement used to be based here. Whether this is the reason for the hauntings may never be known. Witnesses have, however, reported seeing the apparition of a young girl of about 12 years old. She regularly walks across a few of the gardens belonging to the houses in the street, stops as if she is about to enter one of them, then disappears. A good time to see her is late at night, often between 11pm and midnight.

There is also some poltergeist activity in Hillside, although whether this is connected in some way with the young girl is not known. The occupants of and visitors to one of the houses have found themselves locked in one of the upstairs rooms, unable to open the door from the inside. When they have been quite quickly released, as the door was easily opened from the outside, they have expressed a fear of some presence they felt was with them inside the room. Witnesses have also reported that locked cars, parked on Hillside, have had their contents strewn around the inside of the car despite the fact that the vehicle had not been tampered with in any way.

Wimbledon, SW19: The Whitehouse, Windmill Road

According to a report made in the *Wimbledon News* in 1983, a friendly male ghost haunted this building. Witnesses reported seeing the man standing in the hallway. He would turn and look at the witness and then disappear. Other witnesses have reported that one of the rooms is always icy cold, even in the summer months, no matter what they have tried to do to warm it up. They have felt an inexplicable presence in the room.

Wimbledon, SW19: Wimbledon Common

As it probably is in some respects today, 18th-century Wimbledon Common was not a place to loiter after dusk. It was a notorious area for footpads and highwaymen. Jerry Abershaw was one such highwayman who was finally captured, tried and hanged in 1795. Several witnesses have heard and seen Abershaw's ghost astride his phantom horse, galloping across the common.

The actor Edward Silward was one of many people to have seen a strange apparition flitting across their line of sight at night on the common. The various witnesses describe the manifestation as being that of a man who appears to be wearing stereotypical convict's clothing. The ghost runs in front of the witness and then disappears.

Wimbledon, SW19: Wimbledon Theatre, Wimbledon Broadway

This theatre was opened in December 1910 and boasts two ghosts, the first of which is thought to be the original manager, J.B. Mulholland. He has appeared sitting in one of the boxes both during rehearsals and during actual performances.

The second ghost to manifest itself on a regular basis at this theatre is known as the grey lady. She has appeared to a number of different people involved in the workings of the theatre, including a former manageress in 1980. On this occasion the sighting was that of the head and torso of the grey lady who, with a loud laugh, disappeared into the ceiling of the bedroom. Other witnesses have also reported seeing her, fully formed, sitting in the front row of the gallery, passing through locked doors and even frequenting the ladies' toilet. She has also been blamed for the otherwise inexplicable turning on of the theatre's sprinkler system.

Woolwich, SE18

Inexplicable poltergeist activity was the cause of a woman moving out of her council flat in this area of London only months after she had moved into it. The tenant's small child kept looking around the room as if somebody had just entered it and her cat kept running off as if it were scared of an unseen presence. Loud noises and people walking about were regularly heard from the upstairs rooms and one of the bedrooms used to become icy cold for no apparent reason. The tenant reported seeing the shadow of a man on more than one occasion and visitors to the house sensed a feeling of being watched. Despite a great deal of research, there appears to be no possible explanation for the activities, although there are some thoughts that the haunting may be related to a murder carried out either at the flat or in the immediate vicinity of it.

Woolwich, SE18: Fort Tavern, Sandy Hill Road

An unidentifiable misty figure has been seen on more than one occasion in this pub. The haunting is accompanied by the sound of heavy footsteps and a succession of landlords and customers at the pub have heard these even when the figure is not present. There is no explanation for either the footsteps or the figure.

Bibliography

Brooks, John, *Ghosts of London*, Jarrold, 1982

Forman, Joan, *The Haunted South*, Jarrold, 1984

Green, Andrew, *Mysteries of London*, Napier, 1973

Hippisley-Coxe, Antony, *Haunted Britain*, Pan, 1973

Spencer, John and Anne, *The Ghost Handbook*, Boxtree, 1998

Underwood, Peter, *The A-Z of British Ghosts*, Souvenir, 1971

Jones, Richard, *Walking Haunted London*, New Holland, 1999

Index